STARSEED
FOOTSTEPS

RAYMOND GUZMAN

Raymond Guzman/Psychic Medium
Texas, United States

www.raymondguzman.net

Starseed Footsteps/Raymond Guzman. – 1st ed.

ISBN to 978-0-692-14613-2

Art work: Panos Lampridis

DEDICATION

I want to dedicate this book to all lightworkers, psychics,
mediums, healers, reiki masters, and spiritualists out
there. Never be afraid to be yourself and the hardest part
of embarking on a spiritual path is to let go of the fear.
Be authentically you and celebrate your uniqueness.
You are beautiful. Love and light always.

Contents

Chapter 1

The Psychic Call

There are many things that trigger the awakening of an individuals all over the world. I distinctly had known since I was a child that I was extremely different than many others in the spiritual sense. I always felt like I did not click with other children my age and chose to be more alienated as I felt alone even when around others. I always pondered about earth and questioned why I was seeing spirits at such a young age and didn't know if others saw the same things I saw. It wasn't like it just clicked and I had all the answers. No this was beyond normal and it took me many years to realize this was paranormal. I had always felt I had some psychic abilities and I had many experiences. However, one thing I remember that when I was little I would look for coins that others had dropped and would know where to find it. I never asked spirit to show me or guide me but I would just walk towards a specific area and boom it would be right there. Immediately in front of me. I didn't know how this was even possible but if I walked a parking lot. I would look down and see it without any effort. I would feel guided to another area and would continue to find them.

This continued to intrigue me and as I continued to grow I noticed other synchronicities. I would just know what was about to happen or if someone would pass. I never spoke much of this to my mom but I knew deep down inside that there was something different and almost freaky with having these abilities. I do feel in a way that many of the kids who made fun of me and bullied me as a child perhaps picked up on my awkwardness. But I didn't pay too much attention to my abilities and sort of pushed them to the back of my mind thinking this would go away. When I was in my late teens and into my 20's the experiences I had when I was a child lessened more and more. However, I continued to have these experiences but I truly believe when we are adults we have responsibilities and these responsibilities sometimes create these blocks or walls around our consciousness and soul. We are weighed down with focusing on paying our bills for survival and in this we tend to focus less on the most important spiritual part of ourselves. This would be the soul's life path. This is why many starseeds or children who were natural born psychics or mediums often say that they remember having imaginary friends or they used to see spirit but as they grew they stopped seeing or hearing. It is not until something triggers the abilities you were born with and awakens you, that you truly understand or able to answer the psychic call that we all have at one time or another. I know I have mentioned this to some of you before but I remember when I was around 26 and 27 and while working at my job I would be in another part of the building and away from my desk. I had my boss calling me on my extension but at the precise time she was dialing my extension and it was ringing I was silently waiting in the front of her door and she was dumbfounded as to how I had heard it so quickly or how I knew she was calling me. I didn't know why but I would feel this "call" or urge to just walk towards her office. If I had to explain it now, I would say it was as if my soul was being directed by a higher power and I was where I was needed for the specific time and place.

I do believe that we are all assigned where we will work at, who we will have as our bosses and co-workers and this is not just something that is a coincidence and happens. All of this is written before birth and our souls have a say so in what we sign up before. This would be the soul contract. However, I don't want to get off subject so I will go back to explaining this "call." I just knew when something was not right with people. Working with many individuals in a call center environment there is a tremendous amount of positive and negative energy. Energy from your customers calling and those around you going through the emotions. Being empathic didn't help me and I remember many times I would go home physically drained like I had worked out for 5 hours or walked 20 miles with no rest. At that time my job was sitting and doing analytical work so I did walk around as well but the physical exertion was minimal, so there was no logical explanation. I was physically healthy as well. So, this wasn't physical but more on the spiritual side and of course nothing about these gifts made sense to me or even clicked. Thinking back to my childhood I always felt this call and when my mom would take me to the public library I would always go to the metaphysical and occult section of the library. There was like a pull beyond my explanation to do research. Yes, I call it research and I remember being like 8 or 9 years old and would read all kinds of book about witches, mystical, psychics, healers, and much more. I was not your typical or average child. LOL nope this was something that took time for me to grasp. I just knew I was preparing for something. It was as if my soul knew I would be doing this work in my 30's and all the time spent in my younger years was for preparation. If you think about your own life and all the experiences you went through, you'll find some of your stories may be similar to mine. You may have hung out with only the gothic kids, maybe you got your first set of tarot cards, there was something you couldn't explain but it all felt right and like it was sup- posed to happen. This would be the "calling" I am referring to. You don't just wake up one day and say I'm going to buy a deck of tarot cards and do readings or I'm going to be a psychic and do readings. No, everything was in a flow and was a process. It all starts with you being drawn or pulled like a magnet to these things. See the thing here is not everyone is going to be pulled into spirituality or the metaphysical at a specific time. We all acclimate to this or are called towards our duties as light workers.

Now in my early 20's I had my very first spiritual awakening and I believe I was a freshman at college. I was studying business administration and working towards being an office manager or owning my own business one day. So being psychic and helping others spiritually was not even in my vocabulary. During my freshmen year, I began to develop these intense panic attacks or anxiety attacks. I remember I felt like I could not breathe and like I felt pressure on my chest. I remember thinking I'm go- ing to die or have a heart attack. I went to the emergency rooms quite a bit and the doctors would run all sorts of tests and just said you're physically healthy and its just anxiety. They all blamed my levels of stress but I was seeking another answer. I felt something physically was wrong with me and they weren't diagnosing me. You sort of feel lost when the medical world cannot explain what is afflicting you and causing you this anxiety. I learned to control it slowly it went away but from time to time it was very much prevalent. It was as if something or someone was trying to get my attention but I was not able to understand the messages coming at me. All I knew I never wanted to go through this again.

When I turned 31 I was working at this manufacturer company and worked as a scheduler. During my time, there I remember feeling different. I remember one day I walked into that office and said to myself, what am I doing there? I just knew this wasn't the place or job I was meant to do and I cannot explain it. However, being a logical person, I did not acknowledge the calling from spirit or the messages I was already receiving in my soul. I kept dismissing this and continued to work there. I always felt like I didn't mesh with the employees and memories from my early childhood came back. I remember feeling like the 6-year-old who didn't fit in with my classmates. I would see and pick up on things and attitudes from my co-workers and I knew when they were going through something in their life. I knew when they were lying. I just knew things like many of us out there just know things. This was the claircognizance and clairsentience being activated within me. It was the call within my soul that I could not hear or understand.

One day I was sitting in my office all alone while my other co-workers were at lunch and my boss had to run an errand. I remember being there and then suddenly 2 birds both which were doves appeared. Yes, these were doves and they were inside my office. They flew above my head and scared the heck out of me because they were unexpected. However, I remember thinking this was a sign or omen. I didn't know what. I remember they didn't want to attack me but were frantically moving to the front right corner of where I was sitting and would both fly into each other and swooped behind me. I ran to get help to get them out of the office because I didn't want them to get hurt slamming into the walls or windows. Finally, the main door was opened and an employee ushered them out and they flew and disappeared. My co-workers in the warehouse laughed frantically at my reaction to this. I didn't care but I knew spirit was trying to tell me something. I just didn't know the changes that would occur. I remember I kept playing back the birds flying into the office. Then about one week later after this occurred I began to get extremely sick while at work. I would go in fine and then feel these crippling panic attacks and anxiety. I remember feeling my heart was palpitating and feelings like I couldn't swallow. I felt like my throat was shutting down and I remember almost passing out. I would go each day and felt so sick. After about a month the anxiety was so bad that I had to resign. I remember working my last day I was on the phone scheduling an installation and delivery of merchandise and while on the phone I turned pale white and felt like I could not breathe. My boss said somethings not right maybe you should go to the hospital. I said no.... I just need fresh air and she took over my call. I remember going to the breakroom area and just breathing and then I had to leave. It wouldn't go away.

I went to the hospital and thought I was also having a gallbladder attack as I was hurting on my right side where you normally would have pain if you have a gallbladder attack. I remember hearing this voice say you're done. Don't go back. I finally had heard the call but was not sure who this was speaking to me and I also felt this could be just a figment of my imagination. They specifically told me if I went back I would get so sick and would be forced to quit. This was not my calling and not my path. So, while I didn't understand I did not want to get sick again. The next day I wrote an email in which I resigned and although this is not the right thing to do, I had always given in my last two jobs a two weeks' notice. However, this was life and death I was dealing with and my health came before everything. I remember thinking back to those birds that were sent a week before and how all windows were closed and doors and there was no way they could have just flown in and how it was no coincidence that they flew in when everyone in the office was gone. I remember thinking back to how I felt out of place there and miserable and thinking this was not the right job for me.

The more my analytical self, stopped trying to derive to a logical explanation but a more spiritual explanation and then the voice talking to me that I understood the call and knew I had answered that call. The birds were sent by spirit as a sign or omen to me with a message attached. Had I listened to my gut instinct when I got hired, I would have not gone through this. I remember when I got interviewed I knew immediately I would get the offer and be hired. I was later offered the job and hired just like I had believed and known but I wanted to turn down the offer. However, no other offers had become available and bills don't wait. So, I was desperate and took the job knowing darn well I wasn't supposed to. I didn't listen to my intuition and listened more to my fears and worries. After going back and thinking about this more and more the puzzle pieces all came together and this all made sense. I remember hearing spirit say there was too much negativity and negative individuals surrounding me and that once I would leave that job my health would improve. While I believed all of this to be true. My health got worse before it got better. The anxiety attacks continued for months and became more violent. I remember going to the grocery store and getting off the car and walking a few steps and felt my legs were like jelly and so heavy. I felt like I could not walk and I felt vibrations in my legs and while sitting down in the sofa I felt these intense vibrations running down my spine. It felt like these intense electrical currents were moving up and down my spine. I started to have these crawling sensations like when you walk into spider webs or ants are crawling on your skin. This would be primarily focused on my crown area of my forehead. I also felt it on my arms and chest. I would get blurry vision and think wow what is going on. I thought I needed glasses but going to my optometrist only served to be told that my vision was fine and nothing had changed. I continued to feel sick and felt that somehow the person I was in the past was slowly leaving. I was no longer interested in the same activities I had been interested in 2 years earlier. I also noticed that I looked at the world and religion differently. I was always a caring individual but my level of compassion and my senses were more heightened. I remember not being able to eat poultry as I could taste the chemicals used to process the meat. I tasted the additives. During this time my hearing and smell were stronger. I could tell what someone had eaten for lunch. I also remember feeling numb at times and just felt like I was dying slowly but the doctors had no explanation for me. I had never gone through these attacks on a deeper level. Yes, I did think perhaps this was crazy and that I was crazy. It crosses your mind and I didn't have a spiritual advisor or social group to help me through this. I remember praying and learning meditation and this helped me.

Knowing there was no medical explanation I continued to get sick and during a cold February day I remember I was inside of a retail store and shopping. I felt these strong cramps inside my shoulder blades and remember feeling chest pain and breathing was heavy. I felt like an elephant was sitting on my chest and I slowly held on tight to my basket. I remember standing there and felt my heart stop beating it was beating rapidly and slowed down. I remember counting my last two heart beats and thinking I'm going to pass out. I remember seeing pure darkness and this tunnel like a white light and then saw these heavenly skies. I then immediately felt like I was pushed back and in an instant I remember feeling my heart re-starting and the beat was rapid. Extremely rapid and I remember feeling so tired and my mouth was extremely dry. I felt this thirst I could not describe. I had my Near-Death Experience this was my official NDE. It was after this that I was changed both physically, mentally, and spiritually. I would dare to say that this is not even comfortable to talk about even now but if it can help others understand their NDE or people who are awakening then I have served my purpose. I remember knowing I had died for an instant and came back. My purpose here on earth was just beginning and I remember 6 months later I was guided to email this spir-

itual advisor. She explained I was going through a spiritual awakening and how these things I was going through
would dissipate and how new doors would open for me.
She even told me this wasn't the path I was supposed
to lead. She saw me becoming more spiritual and doing
something on the spiritual side of life. That would be my
true calling. After that experience and reading I remember my anxiety and panic attacks left me and the energy
that was surrounding me was one of love. Being united by
a higher power. I felt guided and as if I knew everything
would be okay.

As you can see at one time or another in our life we
are given choices and lessons. However, most of us are
stubborn and do not listen to the calls from spirit. These
calls can manifest in different ways and more importantly
they take you by surprise. They are not expected and they
happen when you are called into this type of work as a
spiritual being. Spirit is constantly speaking to us but at
times we would rather listen to ourselves rather than listening to the universe. But rest assured you will be forced
in one way or another to accept your responsibilities as a
light worker.

Chapter 2

LIFE AFTER DEATH

Dealing with the loss of a loved one is never easy. It's very difficult to process and understand why we are sent to earth and then leave it. To understand this, you must realize this earth is just like a school where we come to learn and study. Our studies are the experiences we have, the pain we endure, the happiness, the accomplishments, the helping and healing we give. I often get asked during medium readings if a loved one can hear them. The answer is YES! Your loved ones are around you and can hear you even if you can't always feel them or see them. Since we are composed of energy, energy cannot be destroyed. Therefore, we only transcend into the spiritual realm which is our true home. Here's some important things to know about the transition from a physical body to our spiritual self.

Upon our passing, the soul is released and the feeling is like levitation. You are lifted up almost feels like flying.

You are usually greeted by loved ones or your spirit guides when you start to cross over. Someone is always waiting for you and you're never alone.

Any health impairments, pain, suffering, anguish that they had before passing is gone and replaced with health and happiness. Our physical body feels pain but our spiritual body doesn't!

A life review is done with our spiritual guides and angels and we see everything we just experienced in the life we had. Depending on our lessons and karma will depend how our soul progresses.

If your loved one showed a lot of anger towards you or hostility they only know love now. The spiritual realm is full of love and peace. Many depictions in movies or media show angry spirits but anger is a human emotion not spiritual emotion. Therefore, they are sorry and learn the lessons they need to know.

They also have school and learn lessons for the progression of their soul on the other side, so they are always busy helping other souls or your family from the other side.

Any thoughts you have of them or if you speak to them. They can hear you. Spirit hears all, knows all, and sees all.

Spirit's main goal is to ensure your happiness so although it's difficult to go on without them, they want you to be at peace and happy.

Spirit can show themselves at any age and look, meaning they don't have to appear in your dreams like they looked like before passing.

Spirit grows in the spiritual realm, so if you lost a child years ago, know they are probably an adult right now. They grow on the other side but it doesn't take human years because spirit has no time.

Rainbows here on earth are glimpses of heaven and signs from our loved ones. Heaven is full of the rainbow spectrum.

Heaven has several dimensions or levels. So just like earth is not the only planet in the galaxy neither is there just one level in heaven. Think of a pyramid that's similar to how the hierarchies in heaven are.

Our loved ones can hold the soul of a baby being born into your family before they come into this world.

We have the choice to reincarnate or stay in heaven. You are given the choice to learn your lessons in a place you feel comfortable and know or come back to earth. Most of us have been here several times before. Hence, the term old souls.

Spirit has no fear. Fear is a manmade emotion.

As a medium we can channel information from them and relay messages. Mediums have an inner light that is open to the spiritual realm and its connection is strongest when we are vibrating at a higher level. Know that your loved ones are at peace and grateful.

Chapter 3

ANTIQUES, USED ITEMS & ENERGY

Most of us have heard of psychometry and this is basically the ability for a person to tune into the energy of an object and tell you about who it used to belong to, years connected, etc. It's a great ability and does require practice but u less you have it developed most people who go shopping at garage sales, consignment shops, antique shops, or thrift shops often are unaware that whatever you buy still carries the energy of the previous owner....

It can be an object like a statue or an old book. Anything that was essentially owned by someone else carries an energy imprint. What's that? Remember we are all composed to energy so when we wear something like a necklace, t-shirt, a dress, or a hat, a piece of our energy stamped to that item. No matter how long it's been your energy is tied to it. So many times, we can feel negative energy if that person was carrying negative energy. A good way to get rid of this energy is to Sage the items. You can also lay clear Quartz crystals on it or any Crystal of preference to clear the energy.

I am very Leary of used clothing and never buy used clothes for this reason. Not every piece that is used is negative but I don't take chances for this reason and because of past experiences. What if the item belong to a person who is now passed? The energy is still there and cannot be destroyed but it can be cleared. I'm not saying you should be fearful and stop shopping at these places but be aware. If you're empathic or HSP be sure to tune into the item you're planning on purchase. How do you feel when you hold it in your hands and then how do you feel when you put it down? That's another good way of testing its energy.

Used objects like statues. My first paranormal experience was my father bringing an antique statue into our home and I saw spirit trapped inside of it. It was a mischievous one too and made all kinds of faces but only I could see it. When I told my mum, she removed the object and the activity stopped. Hence why antiques also can be haunted or full of spirit. Use best judge me and again sage the item if you really must purchase it but not sure of the energy it contains.

Next time you give your clothes away to someone, remember you are also giving someone your energy!

Chapter 4

WHY GIFTED PEOPLE CANNOT READ FOR THEMSELVES?

I often get asked this question and find myself having this issue where I cannot read myself. I can read most people but not myself. I did encounter some colleagues who have said well if you have tarot cards you can read for yourself. My whole issue here is that the level of information you could obtain for yourself would be limited. This is one of the reasons why many psychics get told often if you have the gift why aren't you a lottery winner or rich?

My answer to that is our gifts were designed to help the greater good and also helping humanity but if we were privileged to such information for ourselves how likely would be to follow our spiritual calling and help others? How likely would we experience all the lessons, hardships, here in the physical world that we are meant to experience? The answer is that it's not very likely. While I'm opened minded to receiving information from spirit and guides for myself and my own decision making is concerned. It's sort of limited and they will only share what I need to know but not what I want to know. This is like a spiritual law. So, while using tarot or other forms of divination for yourself may uncover or answer some questions the level and depth of them is not very specific.

For example, if you were to ask Spirit if you are going to move soon and try your pendulum or tarot you may find mixed answers. You might get a yes but when you ask spirit how soon and start mentioning time frames your cards or otherwise may or may not say.

Spirit doesn't work like that and they are limited to telling you things that could alter your life path. Some people have found a workaround and that is accessing the Akashic Records. Because all our blueprints and other life lessons are stored there, psychics, shamans, and yourself can access certain or specific information about your life but again certain information is restricted.

This is why many gifted people turn to others in the psychic community for answers, because we all know about this unspoken rule. Remember if you're needing guidance for yourself, you can use different modalities to get answers or pray for signs or information to be revealed by your angels and guides but there may be resistance encountered. As their purpose is not intended for this. If you are in doubt your best option may be consulting a psychic, medium, healer, etc.

Chapter 5

Soul Agreements and Setting Boundaries

Have you ever noticed that during sleeping you have dreams and travel in your dreams to locations that seem very similar to where you live now or extensively different? Some people all this astral traveling or dimension hopping and the list goes on. Now why this occurs is because your soul learns lessons while awake here in the physical world but also learns and works while asleep. Let's say you wear prescribed single vision glasses in your daily life because your eyesight is no longer 20/20. But in your dreams do you notice that you can see without the assistance of the glasses? Also, you may see everything in color but be colorblind when awake. The reason for this is because the soul is perfect the way it is. We carry GOD within us (The DIVINE SOURCE) and therefore we are powerful spiritual beings, however, before we are born we have soul agreements often referred as (soul contracts, soul blueprints, etc.).

The issue here is that sometimes our agreements have lessons we must learn either in the awakened state (physically awakened) or sleep state (physically asleep).

The problem here is that sometimes we may find as psychics, healers, and mediums that we often wake up more tired than before we went asleep. We may not recognize why we are going through this but if you haven't established boundaries your soul is leaving to other dimensions while you're asleep and causing this draining energy, etc.

How do you know if this is occurring to you? Well if you are dreaming but can't remember the exact dream, or if you felt you were astral projecting or traveling and remain lethargic it's because you have not set any boundaries to your soul agreements. There is a specific set of time on the earthly plane but you can opt to learn these lessons when you want to and how soon. You don't always need to astral travel or dream to learn these lessons. Remember our physical body is a vessel in which we are able to learn and maintain health to stay living here on earth. Sleep time is the only time we get to rest our bodies and mind. If you find yourself in a state where you fall asleep during the day, or just lack energy and feel pain all over and you've ruled out any medical conditions etc., then this could very well be attributed to spiritual travel.

Now as I have mentioned you do have the POWER to set boundaries within your soul agreement. You can simply state "I revoke spiritual access or any astral traveling. I revoke any spiritual influence during my sleep state." This is a technique most developed mediums may choose before they fall asleep to stop spiritual visitations etc. It's like shutting a door to the other sides and dimensions because there are different realities (dimensions) not just earth itself. How effective is this method? It may or may not work depending on how open you are and firm you are about revoking or setting boundaries. Spirits have to follow certain guidelines both earthbound and spirits who have crossed. Other things you can do is have an overactive house full of spiritual activity is to set up clear quartz crystals in all 4 corners of your bed or sleeping area or in all 4 corners of the room where you sleep in. There may be other techniques and explanations but this chapter was designed to just give you a little insight on probably causes and issues stemming from spiritual visitations, lucid dreaming, and astral traveling.

Chapter 6

Transmutation and Self-Containment of Energy

Our energy or Prana (life essence) is a vital part of the human life. However, when we feel powerless or filled with lower vibrations like anger, resentment, jealousy, etc....we are losing or causing energy leakage. Spiritual wellness is essential to all empaths, healers, psychics, mediums, and etc. Being able to turn negative energy or lower vibrations into positive energy and higher vibrations is essentially referred to as Transmutation. You are taking unwanted energy and turning it into wellness for your mind, body and soul. So, what causes us to lose energy or cause a leak in our energy?

Here's a list of energy leaks

- **Obsession** – When you have obsessive thoughts about others or yourself you are losing your energy. Thoughts are energy and therefore you need to align yourself as much as you can to your spiritual self and not with ego. You can obsess about not having money, better jobs, being with a person you want and etc. Think about it, for a second. Let's use an example, you really like this guy but he is already taken. You start thinking he is giving you signals, you start thinking of him, you might start talking to him. When you're at work you can only think of him in your spare time and it consumes your every thought. You have just lost your energy and power. There's healthy thoughts and thinking of someone is not bad but holding onto obsessive thoughts is not good at all.

- **Anger/Retaliation** – You're essentially taking your good energy and thoughts and turning them into negative energy and projecting these thoughts onto others and yourself. Often this not only causes spiritual energy leaks but also can affect your health adversely. This is why people sometimes develop high blood pressure among other ailments. Our body is composed of energy and anything we transmute out into the world can come back and affect you.

- **Fantasies/Habits** – Any daydreaming or fantasies we have about others or habits like dependencies or other habits that are hard to break. We often find ourselves our energy will leak because our mind is fantasizing or using bad habits to cope with life's pressures. This is not only unhealthy for your spiritual self but also for your physical body.

- **Lies** – There's no thing as a white lie. Even if you think your lie harms no one else, it really does...... it harms YOU! Your true spiritual side and true self cannot align with lies. Dishonesty is not something that brings you good energy because you vibrate lower when you do this. Plus, you are putting out negative energy to anyone that your lie touches.

You cannot transmute this energy unless you live in your truth

Sealing any energy leaks is essential to your well-being and in most cases can be done when we focus on healing those areas with positive thoughts. We are all human and no one is perfect. We will always gravitate or fall into one of these categories as the only ones who are not in this are the enlightened beings but we are a work in progress. Infuse yourself with self-love and positive thoughts. Stop obsessions and compulsions. Stop wanting to control within everything that you cannot control.

Deep meditations in which we set all those things aside to work on our self and balance our chakras from crown to root and root to crown we are in control. Energy opens up and allows us to transmute negative energy into positive energy with more fluidity and ease.

Chapter 7

WHEN A CRYSTAL BREAKS: EXPLANATIONS & MORE

Have you ever worn a protective crystal and then all of a sudden it falls and shatters or just breaks on you? There's many reasons for this. Now keep in mind that a crystal's purpose is to provide some type of healing or protective properties against negative or low vibrations. When we speak of low vibrations we are referring to negative emotions that spirits or people carry. Both spirit and humans can carry anger, hate, aggression, disruption, vengeance. When spirit carries this and is around you the crystals are supposed to absorb that energy and transmute it into positive energy. When you say protect what are you referring to? Protecting your energy field. All around our body there are layers of energy fields called auras. These auras are the energy levels you carry around you. Auras can vary by color depending on how you are feeling emotionally. Now going back to the crystals if a living person is harboring some hate for you, anger, thinks it, says it, they are all projecting negative energy from them to you. This can disrupt your energy field. Crystals are supposed to filter this and protect you. However, if that person possesses enough energy and also carries psychic, healing, medium abilities or more they can send this to you. This is often referred to as psychic attacks.

When this happens, the crystal can be on overload and can break. Some skeptics may say this is just a simple accident and it slipped off or just broke because it wasn't sent right to you, that may or may not be the case. Remember there are no things as coincidences.

Here's a list of why crystals may break.

There could be a warning of something that may or may not be negative around you. This could be something that has not yet transpired.

Another reason a crystal could break would be that there was some type of psychic attack sent and the crystal served its purpose to protect you.

There is a magical influence (dark spells) from someone else working against you with a darker energy.

The location you are in (home or property) has high spiritual activity meaning there is too much spiritual energy this could include earthbound spirits, negative spirits, other worldly beings, alien/UFO activity. In most cases there could be a vortex or portal opened to other dimensions in your space.

Messages from your spiritual guidance support team which includes angels, ascended masters, and spirit guides.

The crystal was not meant for you and perhaps was not cleared or cleansed of energy frequently. Remember you are supposed to clear energy from your crystals after buying them and using them ever so often. Every lunar cycle (exposed or buried in the earth during a Full Moon or New Moon), Sunlight, water, and saging them. These are all great methods to cleanse or clear energy they may contain.

Many people ask whether or not the crystals we use are living?

In a sense they carry energy so anything that carries energy could be considered to be living. In my opinion crystals are living spiritual beings of earth (ancient ones) and they might break as well when their mission has been served and it's time for a new crystal to come into your life.

Can I use my crystals if they broke on me?

I would NOT suggest using them or trying to superglue them as the energy departs into the etheric or spiritual realm once this occurs. You could decide to keep them but some people believe it's good idea to bury them in the ground. This is where most crystals come from and it would only make sense for them to return to the ground. A fragment of energy still will remain in the broken pieces that are solid but it's no longer in the intended shape you have received. Some decide to keep them but it's entirely up to you.

Keep in mind this was not written to strike fear or cause you to dispose of any broken or shattered crystals you have. I wanted to shed some light and better understanding on possibilities on why crystals can break. There may be other explanations out there. I hope you find this useful.

Chapter 8

SPIRITUAL TUNE-UPS

When you think of cars you know that after several number of miles your vehicle is going to need a tune up and this could consist of new tires, oil change, etc. The same is true for our spiritual gifts. You see our vehicle is our body and the soul are what receives the tune up. This is often referred to as an attunement.

Why would we need an attunement?

Basically, the universe is constantly evolving and within this matrix or consciousness new knowledge is available, sometimes these are referred to as "codes" and sometimes they are referred to as light energy. The names are irrelevant but what's important is that your soul is constantly channeling from other realms and a higher power. Let me give you an example you have a cassette player and still listening to your cassettes but we now have CD's. Most places have only CD's available but you don't have a CD player! Would you be able to listen to your cassette tapes on a CD Player? NO. You also wouldn't be able to listen to any new music without a CD player or some smart device that has digital media available. The same is also true for our gifts. I'll give you an example, you are a clairvoyant but lately you feel like your visions are not appearing easily. Now with an attunement you noticed another gift or Clair and that's clairaudience. Now you can hear things in your mind telepathically after receiving an attunement. Ah-Ha!

So, you're saying that with an attunement I get a new spiritual gift/ability?

No! Your existing ability could be refined or strengthened or you could open up a new ability.

Can someone give me a spiritual attunement?

No! The attunement process occurs naturally and whoever is sending you healing energy for attunement purposes has to be channeling or a vessel that allows the GOD source or the source of all things to flow into you. So essentially the attunement is coming from the universe. In Reiki sometimes a Reiki master helps you with the attunement process and therefore you're able to learn and accept it. Now attunements can also be done by ourselves without the assistance of a teacher. It's a matter of you being able to connect with the one source of power.

How do I know if I received an attunement?

Just like symptoms of a spiritual awakening you may start to feel certain things days, weeks, or months after an attunement.

- You might feel lightheaded.
- Crown area (top of your head) may feel tingling, strong massive headaches may occur.
- Uneasiness or uncertainty
- Panic attacks/Anxiety
- Dreams may be more lucid or you will receive more spiritual visitations
- You may notice new gifts are now available to you whereas you didn't have these gifts before.
- You might notice any existing abilities you had are now strengthened and have are easier to access.
- Tingles or body temperature changes.

(*It's important to note if you have never had these symptoms you should not ignore this as something spiritual. Always seek out medical advice or get medical attention FIRST to rule out anything health related) If you have ruled out health related symptoms then it will most likely fall into the attunement process.

If you are not resistant to your gifts and in tune with the universe, you will more than likely find the attunement process is very rewarding and filled with love and peace. It will be uncomfortable at times but also a blessing.

Chapter 9

SPIRITS ARE NOT THE LOST & FOUND DEPARTMENT

Being spiritually gifted many individuals will ask for you to find missing items that they have either lost or misplaced. I mean you are gifted with clairvoyance, clairaudience and you have a direct connection to the spirit world so why can't they help you with this? This is a good question.

Many psychics and mediums will not be able to help assist you with this because spirit will NOT participate in something you have lost. Spirit is not a lost and found department. Yes, it may have sentimental value, but spirit is more concerned with healing messages, and providing you with other types of insight that can heal you. Spirit also has duties on the other side such as learning and evolving. In some cases, they will not provide the answer because they are the ones who have caused you to misplace the item or they have hidden it. Some spirits are more mischievous than others and they will hide things. I once had a ring missing and it was a horseshoe ring. You know it had special meaning to me. One morning I woke up and realized it was gone! I looked all over the house top to bottom and could not find it. I even checked in the popcorn box to make sure it wasn't in there. I took each bag of popcorn out and checked and nada, zilch, caput! No trace.

A couple of days later I went to the pantry to get the popcorn box and got the last bag out and would you know my ring was in the box where I freaking looked! Now how did that happen? The ring doesn't have legs of its own and just got up one morning and decided to play hide and seek. This is what I'm referring to in that spirit has the ability to manipulate objects and hide them for a purpose. In most cases if we lose an item it was not meant for us to have. You may spend hours trying to go over your steps but you won't find it. In some cases, your missing item will appear.

Also, sometimes spirit will not assist a gifted individual because they know that you are meant to find your missing item and will. They know at the soul level how careless we are or how much we care about it. Let me give you an example, Patricia has an engagement ring but she takes it off all the time because she doesn't like the stone or wishes it would have been different. She hasn't expressed this to her fiancé or anyone else but deep down inside she hates the ring. One day she cannot find the ring. Spirit knew that she was not attached to the ring and how she really felt. She took the ring for granted. This is why she lost the ring. If spirit assisted her in finding the ring it would not change the fact of how she feels. She would continue to lose it until she expressed to her fiancé how she truly felt. You see, spirit is quite clever.

If you have lost an item, ask your spirit guides for help if they can help you they will.

Chapter 10

HAUNTED OR TO BE HAUNTED, THAT IS THE QUESTION

It's that time of year when some of us like to hit the cemeteries and haunted houses that has a legend or folklore tale attached to it. Perhaps there were tragic events that took place there. Sometimes while doing this we try to prove our ghost hunting skills by stalking these places or going on tours. During this time everyone has their EVP recorders or cameras and flashing pics. Here is the thing you need to understand about hauntings (earth-bound spirits). These are spirits who are stuck here for some reason or another. They truly want to be left alone. Some want assistance to cross over. This was a person who was once living and either stuck reliving how they passed or attached to a place because they feel comfortable there.

We sometimes can take ghost hunting to the next level mainly by what we have seen on popular Paranormal shows on TV. If you are DEMANDING to make their presence known, do not be surprised if you receive scratches or if something physical occurs! Remember just because they are spirit does not mean they do not have feelings. Unless you are contributing and assisting them to cross over you are not helping but making matters worse in certain cases. This is why certain haunted places are known for physical manifestations. Some of these spirits do not even realize they are dead and some were evil in life and will love to play with you. Trust me it's NOT pretty and unless you are spiritually protected you're in for one heck of a ride.

If you are doing paranormal investigations or visiting a haunted location be sure to take some protective crystals with you like black tourmaline, obsidian, selenite, clear quartz, etc. Some herbs like sage, rosemary in a baggie with your crystals is a good idea. A prayer to your guardian angels would not hurt either. Go in with a humble attitude and an open mind. Do not taunt spirit as some things that do not manifest while you are there could actually manifest days or weeks later. They can attach themselves to you and this is sometimes called "piggybacking" and then you become the haunted.

If you are asking questions be gentle and calm and try to avoid demanding or commanding spirits to do your bidding. The "professionals" you see on these paranormal shows have actually had their recaps and they do confess that some tactics they used like demanding or commanding spirits was NEVER a good idea and didn't realize it until they became haunted or things started going bad in their life. Yes, it may be fun and exhilarating to try something like this but again be humble that is my best suggestion for you.

You will get answers when you show love. Also, always try to be with someone and never go alone. Remember you are trespassing their space and they only want respect back.

Chapter 11

SPIRITUAL WARFARE

Within our physical plane (Earth) and beyond there is a spiritual warfare occurring. This is a battle between good and evil and many of us are witnessing this being manifested in what is occurring in the world right now but this is just a distraction to take our thought process away from the bigger picture. There is a divergence occurring with humanity in which we will have to pick a side. Which energy do we claim evil or good?

The last 2 months I have been praying even harder to God, angels and my spiritual team. I have been seeing things shifting. This mainly had to do with Mother Earth and not humanity. For the last couple of weeks, I have seen yellow butterflies and monarchs flying. It's almost like they feel something big is coming and they are trying to escape or others. I sometimes read animals but never insects or butterflies but my guides told me they were a sign of peace but also transformation about to occur and they were fleeing. Typically, we see these where I live during Spring and Summer months, but we are currently in fall as I'm writing this chapter. I also have noticed that birds would always hang around our trees and would be seen around town. Lately it's like all the birds have disappeared as well. I also have noticed the natural disasters are increasing and being more destructive like the earthquakes, hurricanes, flooding and much more. But when we focus on humanity we are noticing that people are turning against one another, innocent people are dying, greed is becoming more apparent and while all this occurring there is two POWERS at be. God (consciousness) and the Dark one (Evil). Now I am not religious but if I believe in God, ascended masters like Jesus and seeing visions of other places I can tell you I am certain there is a dark energy which some may refer or could refer to as the D***l. I don't like to say its name. But let me tell you we are entering a period and have been for some time now that the main war going on is spiritual and it's for souls. As I have discussed in videos and previous writings that this is a wager on souls. The dark side wants as many innocent souls as it can and we as humans are freely giving our souls over to the darkness. It's so easy to understand.

As spiritual beings living a human experience we have a (physical body) or a vessel as some would call it. Attached to this vessel is a soul occupying the vessel and our soul is controlling our body and mind. So, we are a Mind, Body & Soul. When our soul is in a state of rest and love, the darkness has no power! So how does this affect you?

What is going on in your life? What is going on in the world and how are you reacting to this all?

Fear, anger, hate are all states of unrest and lower vibrations. If we are fearing who is going to lead us, if we fear that a war is going to happen then our souls are at an unrest and when we are in a state unrest we start clinging to patterns that we feel calm us but essentially it only harms us. Let me explain let's say you're fearful that your boss is going to fire you. You love food. You will start eating more than you should to suppress your feelings. Now you are a little at ease but this only suppressed, did not get rid of the fear. Hours later you feel guilty for behaving like this and now you're ashamed of yourself. Giving way to another emotion of self-pity. When we are in a state that we cannot control temptation or patterns they continue to occur and turn into addictions. These addictions are spiritual warfare. Our feelings of guilt, fear, self-pity is all spiritual warfare. Now I'm not saying it isn't normal to have these emotions as we are human but some of us live in prolonged states of this and this is where the evil forces can attack you easily.

When you're in a state of love and happiness you are often more targeted by darker forces because you they know you're vibrating at a higher level so with each level in your spiritual path the tests get harder and the attacks get stronger. We must stand strong in our spiritual faith and let go of anything that's bothering us and release it to the universe (God). All things happen with divine timing. Some of us are stuck in a why isn't my life changing now for the better or why didn't I get a promotion or etc. Here's the deal...let's say you got your promotion or the money you wanted before time. You would be prepared for it and the attacks would begin and the temptation (spiritual warfare). Let's say you got an annual pay raise of $10,000 and you got it before you were ready for it...the enemy-

(darkness) would start attacking or tempting you to waste your money on things you didn't need but wanted because you now have money to buy it. But in a few weeks something major comes up and you need the money but don't have it any longer because you spent it all. This is where spiritual warfare comes into place. The divine knew you weren't ready but you tried to push the issue until you got your way. The same thing applies in relationships.

Some people may start dating someone who is married or in a relationship with someone. You know it's wrong with what you're doing by breaking up a marriage or relationship but you try to justify the means because the other person is not happy in their relationship. Does this make it right? NO! You are in spiritual warfare because you know right from wrong but you chose the wrong. Let's say the person you wanted leaves their partner behind to be with you. You got what you wanted right? WRONG!!! You have opened up a can of karma on yourself and chances are that your relationship will not last and this person will do the same to you as you did to them. This is spiritual warfare because your soul will live with this over and over and the cycles repeat over and over until you are in a state of love and inner peace.

When we gravitate towards evil we may feel like everything is coming together but slowly things begin to unravel and what made you happy will now be replaced with destruction and sadness. This is how humanity is affected by temptation and evil. Your soul is affected and is no longer in the higher places where good energy resides. This leaves the doors open for diseases, anger, pain, grief, etc. yes our actions affect our health.

See evil wants you to believe that it doesn't exist and it's just a figment of your imagination so it can have control over the world and subtly get more souls to its side. With every soul who leaves the world in a state of spiritual warfare and chooses darkness over light is helping darkness become stronger. For every soul that is claimed it grows and is able to manifest in our reality with hate crimes, pain, plagues, vulgarity, etc.

In the next few months and into the new year our world is going to see more things we haven't seen before. More violence, uproar, natural disasters, and changes in leaders and in religious powers. All this is part of the spiritual warfare. This is why it's important to not be fearful and love your family or whoever you have, even if that's just you. It's important to do what's right, let go of years of holding anger and resentment to people who hurt you, let go of all that makes your soul and physical body hurt. Pray daily to your angels and call warrior angels down to assist you. Be a warrior angel of the light in all you do. It's not our duty to determine if someone deserves something or not. Be of servitude, be grateful and be love. That's all our planet truly needs at this time.

Chapter 12

SNEAK PEAKS AT YOUR PAST LIFE

If you think this is your first time here on earth you are mistaken. The truth is that many of us are what we call old souls (individuals who have spent many lifetimes here on earth and display a certain level of advanced consciousness). Old souls usually feel disconnected from worldly matters that have no value like money, trends, and popularity. They tend to be more focused on compassion, earthly issues, protecting the environment and much more. If you have found yourself as the black sheep of your family or misunderstood by friends and society you could be an old soul. Most old souls as children display a certain level of maturity or knowingness that adults find intriguing. These types of children may be advanced or talented in areas of art, music, creativity, etc. They may also recall who they were in a past life. They may describe who they were, what they looked like, their name, what they wore, family members, etc. These reincarnated souls are old souls. So, what does this all have to do with sneak peaks at your past life?

At some point in the life you're living right now you may feel inclinations of doing things you wouldn't have thought of doing. You may find that you have certain phobias towards people, places or things. You may also find that certain foods may affect you. You may visit a place or see a place visually and feel connected to the land or area but you have never been there before in your life. Why would this occur? The reason is that subconsciously your soul is aware of these things and will send you signals when you are ready for your soul's evolution. Not many people are aware of the reason why they feel this familiarity. Again, you probably have been there before. It's no surprise some people have phobias like being in water or of heights but why? Sometimes in a past life you may have passed away in that type of environment. For example, someone who has a phobia of water and cannot or will not learn to swim, may have passed in a drowning accident in their past life. Now in their current life they tend to display these intense dislikes for these things or places. You may not understand why but your soul does. You also haven't made peace with this and your soul carries this imprint. Therefore, people who have phobias seek professional help but still suffer from these even if they can mask or temporarily cure them. They may keep reoccurring until spiritual healing from a reiki master or someone who deals with past life regression assists you. Some people seek out hypnotism as form of therapy to deal with this.

You may also see snippets (visions) or dreams of yourself in a past life. You may remember things from your past life or soul mates whom you shared a life with. The reason you are dreaming these things is because when in a dream state, it's easier for your soul to reconnect to these and learn what lessons or things you need to from this to prevent the same karmic lessons or issues form continuing to repeat themselves. Many of us are unaware why we repeatedly keep ending up with the same type of people in relationships that result in us being single and unhappy or why we continue to have the same habits and experiences. If you find patterns are reoccurring in your life this is past life/karmic lessons that are most likely repeating. Until you deal with this appropriately it will continue to happen.

How can I deal with is?

1. Past life Regression
2. Therapy
3. Reiki
4. Past Life Reading
5. Prayers to the archangels (Metatron or Michael)
6. Meditation

These are some of many ways to deal with these things. Again, if you are having dreams you will need to keep a dream journal and write down what you remember (places, colors, smells, conversations, etc.). Information is being shown and given to you to make some peace with all of this.

Some people also have the PAST LIFE SNIPPETS when they first see or meet someone. They may feel like an immediate connection as if when they consider their eyes they know this person but don't remember or can't explain it. This is you recalling this person from your past life. In most cases, you shared a past life together. Sometimes someone from our past life and soul family will come into our life so we can continue the healing we didn't experience in a previous past life. You will feel this calm energy and like this person is the only one who comprehends you. There is a mutual understanding that goes beyond time and space. This is the soul connection and the past life snippets.

Next time you have some feelings or dreams unveiling information you cannot understand or interpret but feels right and feels familiar, these are past life snippets being shown to you. Your soul's memory bank is depositing new information into your memory. While you may not understand this, you will learn to accept or continue your quest for answers. Remember age is only a number for your physical body, your soul is infinite and not defined by a number. Your life that you are living now is only a snippet in the evolution of your soul's existence.

Chapter 13

CHEATERS AND SPIRITUAL BREAKS

It's an interesting concept when you think you have found the person who you would spend your entire life with just decides to either dump you, leave you, or cause heartbreak. However, why do the people you have trusted the most often hurt you the worst? They were your soulmates or at least you thought they were and now your world is shaken up and torn apart.

While we all have a blueprint, we design and work with our guides and spiritual guidance team before being born into this life and existence, that same blueprint contains exit points not only to leave the world and return to the spiritual world but also contains exit points in your free will and areas of LOVE. We all heard that certain people become a lesson, experience or lesson learned. This is all part of our spiritual evolution and growth. However, you must understand the reason why your spouse, partner, boyfriend, or girlfriend has cheated on you. Was it something you did? Was it temptation? There are too many reasons why they could have done this but one of the main reasons is that the partner is seeking some type of healing that they can no longer find in themselves or in you. This is one of the main reasons why people cheat on one another. See every partnership provides you with physical and spiritual healing.

This doesn't justify the fact that they hurt you and did this as it's not spiritual and is a lower vibration for them but most cling to these relationships even when knowing the truth for the sake of a security blanket. It could be several things stemming from the familiarity of having a partner, shame of what others will think, financial reasons, and the list goes on. Remember the universe knows your intentions and this is where the lessons are. The longer you cling to a person who has chosen to be with someone else, the more pain you create for yourself and you are shutting yourself out on the blessings the universe has. Some are afraid that they will not have the willpower or strength to survive this separation or turmoil but in most cases, you will be just fine. It's the FEAR that holds you back.

Another reason why relationships go bad is based on the intent and I am going to go into more depth. If you met someone who was physically attractive and that is your only reason wanting to be with them, then your relationship will more than likely not last. **Listen to this carefully, YOUR RELATIONSHIP HAS NO LOVE!** Yes, you may love their body but that's not loving your soul and anything that is not true or genuine for your soul is not part of your destiny or life path.

Next you may be with someone only for their money. Yes, what attracts you is the security of having a home and money. Yes, you may work but having a partner who is financially secure and stable is very enticing. However, deep within your heart you don't truly love them. You may trick yourself into thinking you do but your soul knows the truth. Therefore, relationships go sour quickly or after some time. Money and having a place to live doesn't mean anything if you are unhappy spiritually and physically unable to feel love by the other person.

Another explanation would be karmic lessons that you MUST now learn from a past life. Some of the reasons I mentioned above may be what you did in a past life and now you are reaping those karmic lessons and having to experience them in your life now to move further and acclimate to the next level in your spiritual growth.

Sometimes the reason this person has cheated on you has nothing to do with this but rather just lower vibrations of lust, and spiritual bondages that they do not know how to get out of. Spiritual attachments can also lead to this and can drive others apart. So, like I have mentioned there are numerous reasons why people cheat.

If you are consulting a psychic, medium, or healer and obtain a reading and this comes up or your specifically ask them if your partner is cheating. Regardless of the answer you are given your soul already knows the truth and you should not attack the reader or feel they are lying. In many instances your soul asked this because a certain level of your inner intuition is telling you that there is reason and validity here. Your soul doesn't let this idea go and it repeats in your mind and in your heart.

While this may be negative news, we are just messengers and do not have control over what spiritual messages are given. An important lesson here is that Spirit will always tell you what you need to hear, and not what you would like to hear. Also, keep in mind there are different levels of cheating ranging from ideas, thoughts, actual physical, verbal, flirting, social media (online), and the list goes on and on.

The good news is that in some cases these riffs can be amended and healed if both partners are willing to work together and remember the reason they came together as one person. Prayers, counseling, forgiveness are sometimes band aids and the real healing will come from the soul level and both recognizing there are parts of you that still need healing or need each other.

Remember there is always something deeper in every relationship where one partner has cheated and hurt the other. It's not as cut and dry as they just cheated on you. There's a lesson, a growth, and evolution in all of it.

Chapter 14

PREPPING FOR THE 6TH DIMENSION

If you are on Facebook or have some other form of communication, you already know the universal shifts are taking place. The shifts are not just changes in our reality here on earth but at the spiritual level (your spiritual self) and the universal consciousness. For many who are still stuck vibrating at the 3rd and 4th dimensions you may have noticed that you are still shocked by humanity and what is occurring in our world. Some are just beginning on their spiritual path and awakening. This is what we are seeing in our world as chaos. This is what social conditioning and propaganda has done to our consciousness and to a certain extent we have become divided as humanity on earth. If you are vibrating at a higher level and tuned in with your higher self you are noticing how worldly matters do not affect you the same way as others or it doesn't surprise you because deep down you know everything has happened with a purpose behind it.

As we move into the 6th dimension you are going to notice many things happening in our physical plane (earth) and to yourself (physical body) in response to the universal codes and universal shifts in consciousness occurring.

Let's first a look at what will happen here on earth as we shift.

Earths 6Th Dimensional Changes

- Human Behaviors- Those still vibrating at old dimensions will be the ones spreading hate, anger, violence, depression, committing acts of violence but not knowing why they did this, taken by surprise by social or legal changes occurring,

- Mass Exodus – People will leave this planet either by natural causes (disasters) or accidents and all will happen as it's written. We will witness these first hand and not understand why this had to happen. Remember we never truly die as energy cannot be destroyed but many will opt for this exit to return HOME (Spiritual Realm aka Heaven).

- Weather Patterns (Hurricanes, Fires, Tornados, Tsunami, Earthquakes, all epic proportions and will seem like these are the end of times).

- Solar Flares and Global Warming, these will occur more frequently and affect our animals here on earth and plants (crops). Certain species will become extinct if they are already close to extinction.

- Earth's winters and summers will become more intense!

- Something will be witnessed in the sky and this will occur at night and be like the aurora borealis but way different. This will be well documented and will occur within the next year or so.

- Earth will sing (Meaning the strange noises and ringing we as star seeds, earth angels, spiritual people have already been experiencing.) The earth does feel love and pain and she will sing for us so we can hear this and be made aware. There will be strange sounds occurring in different parts of the earth.

- Your pets and any animals will become more sensitive to these changes and may exhibit weird behavior themselves. They may become shy or afraid at times, their energy will shift.

- Ascended Masters will start appearing (yes I know you're probably thinking really?) The Blessed Mother, Jesus, St. Germain, and other illuminated beings who had the ultimate ascension and transitioned to the higher realms of consciousness will be working with many light workers and will appear or make news as they leave proof or revelations as I would like to call it here on earth. Yes, they are not a made-up fairy tale and are very real.

- Faith - Our faith in the universe will be tested and more people must choose a side of darkness or light. Good vs. Evil this is a battle and you cannot hide in your home and ignore this. You will be given an ultimate side to choose and we always have but now more than ever you will need to prepare because those who choose darkness will be affected and impacted more greatly than those who chose the light. The darkness will the (war, the violence, the hate, the division, and the disease.

- The Political System – The government we know will be different and not represented the same way. We will see shifts within structure and many people come and go. The people will uproar and focus on seeing the change we seek. Some states and countries will revise their laws.

- LGBT Community – There will be some scandals around this and hate crimes may be witnessed but there are going to be more riots and protests for the fighting of equality. Does this mean the laws passed for marriage (yes) but there will be more riots?

- We start seeing a shift in people's attachment to their technology and a re-emergence of more simple times. This does not mean technology will go away but we are almost enslaved to our technology. People in the 6th dimension will let these tendencies go! We will see everyone coming together more and more love slowly emerging.

- Marijuana Laws – I also see laws changing in this area and also destruction of mass farms which harvest and grow this plant.

Now we will look at the changes we will experience as humans:

- Astral Travel – Those who astral travel will notice that their tendencies increase to travel to other dimensions.

- Spiritual Awakenings – These will occur in people who were born 1980's and some older generations will start to experience new waves of spiritual growth or seek the truth outside of the regular doctrine or belief systems imposed on them.

- New Wave Hippies – We had a wave of people who were labeled as hippies but really were all about love for our planet in the 60's and we will see more people becoming more involved in the movement to promote peace and happiness on earth.

- Changing of eye color- There will be a new eye color or mutation of genes in the DNA of humans and will make an appearance. This is the extraterrestrials working on our DNA and evolution of humans here on earth.

- Telepathy – There are going to be people who have this gift dormant and notice it awakens. This will be mental communication between people.

- Cell phones will be evolving and new technology introduced but operates like a projecting on surfaces. I get this will be small and somehow incorporated into watches maybe into jewelry as well.

- Human Intelligence – There are going to be expansion and new inventions and cures developed for certain type of cancers.

- Self- Healing Abilities – We are going to notice these changes as well. We will rely less on medicine and more on ourselves and nature for cures.

These are just some of many more things to come but too much to mention here. Many of us are awake and ready for the 6th dimension and it will be our duty as lightworkers to help others shift into the new level of consciousness.

Chapter 15

EMPATH WOUNDS

As empaths, psychics, mediums, and healers we may not realize that the energy of others can affect us not only physically but also spiritually. Since we are highly sensitive people (hsp) and able to connect with others emotions they can latch onto the person who is tuning in. If you are beginning your spiritual journey as an empath, you may feel suddenly like the emotions you are carrying are not yours. These could feel out of place and not the norm. Sometimes we may not even realize we are a different person spiritually until a loved one mentions to us that our personality or energy seems off or different. Although our soul is composed of energy and cannot be destroyed, it can still make us feel emotional pain because our soul is not free but in a vessel (our human body) which transports it. When we are tuned in, there isn't a manual to control what or who we feel energy from, so this is where we can suffer empathic wounds. These are energetic imprints that are absorbed by the person who is an empath.

You may feel/do the following.

- Extreme Moodiness
- Sadness or deep sorrow
- Anger, Hate, & Resentment
- Pain
- Frustration
- Low Self Esteem
- Attachment
- Spiritual Bondages (addictions)

The list can go on and on. The empathic wounds will heal but you must find out whose energy you have absorbed. In many instances, it will be the people you were last around or who may have low vibrations and emanate the things mentioned above. Now some empaths may carry this energy for prolonged periods of time and when they do it creates a wound/scar in their energy and soul. It can cause the person to become more vulnerable and have issues letting go. This is frequently seen in people who have been in hurtful relationships but they still love the person and think of them even when they are already in a new relationship and with someone new. The pain isn't very easy to go away nor are the feelings.

What do you do if you have empathic wounds?

Here's some tips to help you start the healing process.

- Think self-loving thoughts about yourself and others

- Maintain distance from the person who has caused your empathic wounds
- Remove anything belonging to this person because even if they are gone their energy is still tied to their belongings.
- Sage
- Do a bath in salt as this will help cleanse and purify your aura.
- Say daily affirmations
- Prayer to the archangels specifically Metatron
- Meditation and relaxation
- Letting go of the need to be in control or fearful of the future
- Know you are powerful and in control of your own destiny
- Think positively as you will attract what you believe to be true to you

If the pain continues then you may need to be more direct and get some closure from the person or people who have caused these wounds. Try to understand why things had to happen as they did or why there is now pain instead of joy. Many resist the healing and hope that things will fix themselves and this is where the trap begins and injury to our souls occur leading to empath wounds. Remember we are not victims of any situation but we are spiritual warriors. You have the keys in your hands.

Chapter 16

CLOAKED SPIRITUALITY

We have spiritual people and then we have those who are cloaked in spirituality. As I embarked on this journey I have seen so many things in the spiritual world of psychics, mediums, healers, and I'm sure I will witness more as time progresses. For those of you just starting out on this path you have yet to experience the many ugly sides of spirituality. Yes, not all is sugar coated and rooted in the light. We do have quite a bit of "professionals" and I use the term loosely who pretend to be spiritual but are talking about someone behind their back, sees everything as a competition, their way is the only correct way and the list goes on and on. But why? Why are there so many people who strive to bash other professionals like them? It sometimes boils down to jealousy of your fellow colleague or better yet a rumor or rumors spread by others to discredit or bring your image down.

Most of us are so quick to listen to rumors that others spread but rarely do we consider the source and most of the times we believe everything that is fed to us by others because we tend to give the benefit of the doubt. The thing with spirituality is that it's not enough to have the name attached to you. Yes, we do carry titles as psychic, medium, and healers to identify our abilities but spirituality carries no labels. A true spiritualist will not try to stop someone from their path to help others. There is no judgment. Only ego and those who are cloaked in spirituality will do this.

People who are cloaked in spirituality try to set up rules on how things should be done in a controlled environment or they find themselves with some authority or position and they become power hungry. Sometimes they are not sure if they are doing things to elevate their image or to do a good deed. They are usually torn on what is the right thing to do. They may be well versed in the subjects of spirituality or modalities but the one thing they cannot change is their intentions and energy. As I've said before you can easily identify who is doing their line of work for spirituality, popularity, or etc. They preach love but yet they judge others. It could be that the person they are bashing is spiritual and has attained some level of success in their field that they have been unable to attain. Much of this all boils down to ego. Those who are cloaked in spirituality tend to refute the fact that they can be wrong or they can still learn. They truly do not want to learn or think others could teach them something else. They may attack people at first by trying to impact their job, clients, or make excuses with no validations once so ever.

The fact is that when we deal with psychics, healers, mediums the world of spirituality has set up courses, modalities, techniques all positive to help others tap into their gifts or further develop the gifts of others. The problem with this is when those spiritually cloaked try to set ways of reading others or trying to discredit others on their methods of doing readings. Everyone's gift is different and unique and you cannot tell someone that the way they are doing readings or healings is wrong and this is the "way" that is the "correct" way of doing things. Spirituality does not work like that. Many people who are spiritual light workers process and receive messages differently. There are people who use their gifts to channel, some receive messages or sense things, others may speak solely with their spirit guides, and you have others who speak with their angels to relay messages. When we consider things like evidentiary perspective of psychic or mediumship readings things may not connect immediately as everyone reads differently. Sometimes the information will not resonate with the sitter immediately because their mind is overwhelmed with what they just received or they are thinking hard to put two and two together. It is sometimes after a reading that days, weeks, or months later the reading will resonate or things will truly click.

There are others who will immediately be able to validate information given. It does not mean that the reader or spiritual person is wrong, but what is wrong is when those cloaked in spirituality try to discredit another reader or another person for their own purposes. Their connection with spirit is different than another person. We all have our own ways of relaying messages and it doesn't make it wrong.

One area is future insights sometimes they will not manifest until the future so it's hard to validate or feel the connection, this does not mean the reader is wrong. You also have to keep in mind that with any reading we are just messengers for spirit. Some of the information you have received can be altered or changed by you because of your FREE WILL. What we get are energetic snapshots of what we are being told or able to see within the confines of the gift we have. This is a great misconception where many sitters believe their reader was wrong because they didn't see the things mentioned occurring. Sometimes they will not occur because the reading actually was positive for you and propelled you forward to make those necessary changes to avoid what the reader saw during your session.

Spirituality does not come with a manual and does not have a certain set rules or ways of doing things. When we start to put spirituality in the box we are deviating from spirituality into ego. Spirituality is not a cloak we wear or pair of hats or shoes. It is a chosen lifestyle, it's who we are and we live and breathe it every moment of our life. This doesn't mean spiritual people do not drop the cuss words, get angry, defend themselves or go through the same emotions as others. After all we are spiritual beings living a human experience. Spirituality is love and acceptance of others.

To those who have ever been a victim of a spiritually cloaked individual who has caused you drama or some type of upset, know that KARMA is watching and everyone in this world and the next reaps what they sow. Be sure to plant seeds of love and remove the ego, the judgement, the hate. Love is the only way forever and always.

Chapter 17

TUNING INTO SPIRIT WITH DISABILITIES

A big misconception is around people with disabilities and this could range from a physical or mental standpoint. Our gifts tend to become stronger when one of our 5 senses are compromised or if we go through some type of medical trauma or situation that transforms our live on a deeper level. When we consider people, who suffer from autism, ADHD, or other condition we may think they are not able to tune into the spirit world or they may make comments to us and we pass them off as being in state of mental illness or etc. While science continues to make progress with many medical diagnoses there are numerous cases reported of the wrong diagnosis or cases in which spirituality is involved and there is no scientific explanation that can be placed.

So, what I'm getting at to be more precise is that those who exhibit signs of autism or have it and those who may suffer from mental illness if they are telling you things that you may not be able to understand like they are telling you that they are seeing people in their room, but you can't. Or they see other worldly beings but you can't. Don't ignore them but take them as being serious.

Essentially, we are all so busy and glued to the matrix we live in and in this we see everything cut and dry and form a logical standpoint. However, anyone who is spiritual and has had their own spiritual experiences can tell you when they had their experiences whether it was a haunting or some other form of paranormal experience that they were not thinking about this or even expecting it to happen. It just happened. But many times, when psychics or mediums are tuning in or channeling information a part of our brain that is unused is switched on and there are some studies being done that shows us in that moment a part of our brain is working but science may or may not see activity.

Those who are suffering from a physical disability either eye sight loss, hearing loss, touching, tasting, we all have had to rely on our other senses and strengthen these senses. Like those who are legally blind may not be able to see with their eyes but their intuition is very much on point and if someone enters the room they can hear them. So, their hearing developed further. With psychics, mediums, and healers we have essentially tuned into our extra sense (intuition) and rely on it at times. With those who are mentally or physically challenged they have disconnected at times from their immediate surroundings and their consciousness or spiritual side emerges making them more sensitive to the spirit world. So, some people who have worked in psych wards may have found that there are patients who talk to people or things that the workers cannot see. Or they may tell you something that you think that there is no way for them to know but it makes sense or resonates with you on a deeper level. These individuals may have medical conditions but this doesn't inhibit or stop their connection with the spirit world. They are in fact more in tune than some of us and are very sensitive to what they see.

Spirits have an easier time manifesting around any-one with a physical challenge as well and may see them as targets for attack or to get the families attention. If you have any one who has some challenges and they are going through some paranormal issues, just know there's more to what you or others can see. Spirit is always around us. I'm not saying that you should ignore medical advice as that should always be taken seriously. However, from a spiritual standpoint anything that a doctor cannot explain or cannot diagnose may be something on a spiritual level that should be considered and looked at more deeply.

Chapter 18

SYMPTOMS DURING THE MOON CYCLES

During the different phases of the moon you might feel many physical differences. Believe it or not the lunar cycles strongly impact our physical and emotional aspects. We are all part of the universe and interconnected as I've explained in other chapters. There is an invisible grid of energy that looks like a spider web. Whatever vibration is going through the universe at any given moment can set off a chain of events and change our behaviors. Humans and animals feel it the strongest. Let's take a further look at what is felt and some of the affects.

FIRST QUARTER SYMPTOMS:

• During this lunar cycle you might strongly emotional, depressed, relationship issues may surface, you might feel utterly challenged to accomplish tasks. You might have more headaches, anxiety, spiritual awakening symptoms may be felt stronger.

The Do's and Don'ts:

• Do initiate ideas, proceed with any thoughts, be positive,

- Don't change your mind, pause and reflect, pro-crastinate

FULL MOON SYMPTOMS:

During this lunar cycle you might feel things more intensely. You might feel others emotions strongly, arguments may ensue, you might feel extreme shifts between happiness and sadness. You might even be melancholy. You may notice the behavior of others and express how you feel. Goals or wishes might be fulfilled. This is also a perfect time for haircuts as rumor has it that your hair will grow faster. LOL, but aside from that you might feel stronger hunger, spend more money, treat yourself, shopping for new shoes, and make a certain trip. You might find your stamina is stronger and physically you have more energy.

The Do's and Don'ts:

- Do complete ideas, put finishing touches to any project, and be proactive. Go outside and look at the moon. Set crystals out under the moonlight to charge.
- Don't keep secrets, sign contracts, gossip, initiate rumors, and over indulge.

LAST QUARTER SYMPTOMS:

During this lunar cycle you might find yourself with more sympathy and compassion for others. You might forgive them for things that have hurt you. You might speak to an ex or reconnect with someone from the past. It's all about clearing the air and fixing what's broken in our life. You should reflect on what needs healing and focus on putting the pieces together again. You might feel less hungry and some physical changes may occur like loss of water retention, and possibly easier to lose some extra pounds if you're dieting.

The Do's and Don'ts:

- Do release any negative vibrations and energy you have held on to. Release any pain and move on. It's all about you purging yourself spiritually to reconnect with the truth. Cut the spiritual cords.
- Don't hold on to negative feelings, seek revenge, hurt others, and be bitter.

NEW MOON SYMPTOMS:

During this lunar cycle you may initiate change, make goals, brainstorm. During this time, you need to set proper intentions for your life. Where do you want to go, do, etc. You might be more anti-social during this time, catch up on things you've been holding off on. You might experience more episodes of insomnia and restlessness at nights. Especially if you are psychic, you already know we wake up during the night time numerous times but you might feel it stronger during the New Moon. You might feel your nerves are on edge a little more than normal. Lucid dreaming may be more prevalent.

The Do's and Don'ts:

- Do hold back from being around large crowds if you are empathic as you might feel shy. But if you're okay it's perfect to mingle with small group of people you know. Drink more water, exercise, eat healthy.

- Don't do much social or public speaking, make sudden decisions, and don't say things without carefully considering the impact of your words.

Sort of keep a lunar journal and write down the things that occur to you during the lunar cycles and notice any patterns or trends that occur. This will give you a good insight as to what to expect emotionally, physically, and spiritually

Chapter 19

THE TWIN FLAME FRENZY

I can't tell you how much the Twin Flame topic has come to the forefront and in recent years but let me start by saying. When I was around 7 years old I told my mom what if I had a twin out in the world like me. Someone who talked like me, looked like me, etc. Lol thinking back I had a HUGE imagination but I still like to think I do. But this always stayed with me until my spiritual calling and path took place and I remembered uttering those words. I guess I knew I have a twin flame out there. I have seen my twin flame but have not made a connection but let me explain further the questions around this concept.

First thing is why is a twin flame called a flame was my question? The answer was that the spiritual union between two like souls is an intense spark of energy and when they are together the synergy can be often seen like a flame. A flame carries no shadow. If you don't believe me light a match stick and hold it against a wall or surface it holds no shadow. Hence the term flame...the twin flames hold intense light and both are lightworkers usually. Together as one they can easily bring light stronger than by themselves into this world. When together they both shine spiritually like a flame and the energy is quite intense.

Twin flames often dream of this person, feel this person, meet this person, or never meet this person but still feel them or see them in dreams. You don't have to know this person to feel them. In my case I have always felt I had a twin our there but I didn't know it was called twin flame.

The twin flame isn't every soul in the planet. Meaning not all people have twin-flames. If you have a twin flame it is most likely karmic bonds and patterns you both had to learn in a past life but for some reason failed to master and so you're given a chance to work together or at least feel the energy of the twin to work out your life lessons.

You don't have a half soul and the other person has half soul. That's nonsense and yes we all have our own souls, but you have what I call more like a spiritual marriage or bond. So essentially if feels like your other half.

Twin flames can be in a different part of the world, and still work together at a vibrational and spiritual level. Because twin flames have telepathy most of their lessons can be done while in sleep mode or dream time. Since our souls can transcend space and time the union is usually in dreams, although you can meet in person.

If you're lucky to meet your twin flame the relationship will be plutonic and often very intense emotions that you feel the connection so strong that you both flee. Yes, the love of your twin flame is so intense you can literally go to battle with words, find their other half is so much like them and they get scared. One twin doesn't have to be present to know or feel the others thoughts, emotions, so they often know if secrets are being kept.

It is rare for flames to be couples and because of their intense relationship they often remain more of friends bonded but rarely are the relationships fruitful or last. Usually twin flames will be in their own relationship and still think of their other half or have jealous feelings about them. They might even cheat on their current partner to have a moment with their twin flame. Again, if you are lucky to meet yours.

Most people who have twin flames see the angel number 11:11 because this frequency is a spiritual call at the soul level. So just like angels and ascended masters use this number for messages....11:11 is often a synchronicity among twin flames. When you see this number know that your twin flame sees it too! 11:11 adds up to 4 and 4 divided by 2 souls who are twins is 2! So, there is like a code among twin flames. I see 11:11 a whole bunch. Now some may not agree with me on this concept and again I don't expect you too...but my guides and angels have explained this. I share this information humbly.

Twins may also go through their spiritual awakenings or lessons at the same times and crave more teachings and information.

The lessons carried out by twins is to leave an imprint in this world and change it for the better. You both learn your lessons together.

Most flames are givers and give so much time and energy to others. They are usually selfless and love their families unconditionally but always love their other half as well.

You will know when you have met your twin flame or if you have one because the energy is very well defined and cannot be confused. You'll just know.

Chapter 20

Twin Flames Part II: The Chase and Run

Now I had covered that the twin flames some-times come together and unite or spend some time during this life time but for whatever reason they separate. In most cases the reason is the similarities in personalities is like staring into a glass mirror. This can cause you to have that moment of feeling like this person is so deep and knows you better than yourself. While this is all fine and dandy, many of us fear others knowing our thoughts or not having some level of privacy.

There are several phases that Twin flames who come together in this life experience and I will outline them here.

Plutonic Phase- The relationship may start off very plutonic with strong surges of romance or attraction for each other but slowly this is replaced with control and protectiveness. Think about it for a second you and this person have shared many life times before but there is some unsettled business or periods of feeling rejected. When you are with someone who may have hurt you in a past life you may or may not remember this or if you have been apart and had other partners, they may always hold this against you. They might not be able to accept your past and come to terms with it. In fact, many twin flames will notice this is one thing that draws them apart. It's a topic that keeps repeating itself and eventually leads to arguments.

Chase Phase – Some twin flames may be with other partners and still find that they are chasing the twin flame while in a relationship. So, some of these twin flames deal with feelings of guilt or depression. They know subconsciously or at the soul level as to who is their twin flame but they don't want to break up their existing family. This is where infidelity takes part in existing relationships and one twin may not want to wait or will put pressure on the other twin to leave their family or past behind to start over with them. Essentially this is like a rubber band which is stretched to its fullest capacity and eventually busts. Some twins leave or break up their families to be with the one who they love but if they have children from a previous relationship often struggle with depression or guilt thinking about what they had to do and the sacrifices they had to make, to be happy.

Run Phase – This is one of the phases in which one twin flame is very surprised with the intensity of the relationship and decides it's too much. They run and once they run this can result in one or both twins going separate ways to recharge and decide what they want to do. Some reconcile and come together again to give a second or third chance but others just go and never look back.

Again, I will stress that some of these twin flames meet in this lifetime for karmic reasons and unresolved issues so it's rare they stick together like soul mates do. If both twin flames will stick together they will always have arguments, there will be seeds of doubt, but the flame of love burns and forgiveness is always there. If twin flames have separated in most cases they may meet their soul mate and still think about their twin flames.

In some instances, the twin flames are psychically linked and therefore distance does not matter and they can sometimes telepathically communicate with one another. Dreams may occur when one twin is thinking of the other.

If both twins fight hard enough to stick together there must be constant reminders of the love for each other and this will need to be expressed as actions. Trust is something that must always be there and forgiveness as well.

Some twins cope with the intensity of the relationship by making promises and remembering them. Some may decide to do activities like reiki on one another to heal those emotional or spiritual parts of their soul that still needs healing and acceptance on. Some twins eventually spend a very long time apart and then remember that there was a reason they came together and communication may commence. Twin flames will need to cope with any jealousy because if the twins have found each other and one is in an existing relationship it will tear and hurt the other twin. They will need to have some kind of involvement in their life.

If you believe you have found your twin flame you should not give up on connecting with them and there is always hope. If you cannot be together, this is not your fault and dispose of this guilt. In some scenarios when twins are asleep they are together in the spiritual realm so while you cannot or may not be able to be together in your physical life, your souls are always connecting and that may be enough.

Chapter 21

A SPIRITUAL VIEW ON GOD

Being a clairvoyant and spiritual medium, I often get asked what my take on GOD is. I was once asked if my gifts were from GOD or did I get them from another source. I was drinking a cup of tea of course and almost spit it out as I thought the question was sort of silly but then I thought about why this person was asking. After some thought it does make sense why they asked this. Some people tend to work through spirit, the light, GOD, angels, and the heavenly spiritual realm. You have some though who do have abilities but use the dark side of it and it is not GOD who they believe in and they use the lower spiritual realms for their information as a source. Having years or researching, reading, and just knowing the difference between good and evil, her question made absolute sense.

I was raised as a Catholic and later Baptist but it wasn't in religion where I felt my complete wholeness as a person. I do believe and respect the doctrine but it never felt quite right all the stories mentioned and written by man. I later found my own spirituality and calling as I like to describe it. Now being spiritual does not mean I don't believe in GOD because I most certainly do. I don't like being categorized into a place of whether I do or don't or I'm being too religious for believing this or that. My truths are what I have experienced, witnessed, my connection to angels. First off let me tell you I am a child of GOD and I do believe in this spiritual being. I don't refer to GOD as being a male or female because GOD has no gender. GOD is an existence of LOVE! GOD is all powerful and we carry a little piece of that love in our DNA and our soul. I don't believe GOD has a physical body but is the universal energy that has been here from the beginning of time. I don't believe my gifts come from any other place or it could be possible without GOD.

I know some who are spiritual or follow another belief system or religion may say well this is impossible because some religions condemn people like us who are spiritualists, mediums, clairvoyants and healing. They call it a work of the DEVIL. Some may even say; how can you be spiritual if you believe in GOD? See, spirituality doesn't mean you deny the existence of GOD but instead you are open to all possibilities. I also believe in the Blessed Mother Mary since she did appear to me in a dream 2 years ago. I also believe in many figures from the different doctrines.

Do I believe there is a DEVIL? Yes, but not like how it's depicted or stated in the doctrines. This too is an energy and consciousness. I don't believe we carry that in our energy or soul at all. However, being in a world that is not our true home there is a constant battle of souls. Like I've mentioned before there is a greater battle going on behind the scenes. This is a spiritual battle and a battle of souls. We all have a side to choose one of dark or light. I have chosen the light and will always believe in GOD and the angels. I have had too many experiences including being touched by an angel. I have seen the lower levels of the spiritual realm and the highest levels and so yes Heaven (Higher level in the spiritual realm) and Hell (Lower levels in the spiritual realm). Yes, they are very present, and the spiritual realm is a like a tier or a pyramid. The levels go up from the lowest to the highest. Not everyone makes it to the very top until they do go through several reincarnations and spiritual development.

But going back to GOD. Everyone can believe in GOD and you should not feel ashamed because you are a psychic or medium. Even if we are condemned or misunderstood so what? Jesus was misunderstood by many and labeled as a false prophet in his time. He was crucified per the doctrine but he was always true to himself. He always said he received messages from his father GOD. GOD was a spirit or energy so therefore he was able to see and hear what others in that time may have not been able to. Jesus was a medium. He could cast out demons (meaning he knew and could identify lower level energies). He was a healer and could heal the blind and heal others. He was truly remarkable but labeled and bashed. So many thousands of years later and people still bash us for what they don't understand. Insane, right?

So, if there is GOD why do bad things happen to us and why do we live then die? First, you never truly die. We are energy and we only go back to our true kingdom which is the spiritual realm. This is a temporary experience here on earth. GOD doesn't allow bad things to happen. We signed up for these lessons before coming to earth and being born in this life. We may not remember and therefore many people blame GOD for the misfortune in the world. Would you blame yourself for not passing a test? If you answered NO, you are being truthful. Those of us who are not spiritually awakened always seem to blame someone else and never take responsibility for our own mistakes etc. When we cannot understand why a situation turned out in our favor we start to blame others, circumstances but never truly accept responsibility. Many of these diseases are created by humans here on earth and by ourselves. You see those of us who are vibrating at lower levels full of anger, hate, and evil tend to see those areas of our bodies or chakra's affected. Let me paint an example, let's say you have a lot of heartache and hate for someone in your heart and spend years holding grudges without being able to forgive that person. It would not surprise me if years later you start being affected with heart issues or cardiovascular issues due to the blockage in that one area of your heart chakra. The energy blockages we carry are partly responsible for the issues within our human body and the reason why physical death occurs. The other factor is our environment and our soul's blueprint (contract). This is all temporary. Just because bad things occur in life and in the world does not mean GOD doesn't exist.

There are many of you out there that may not necessarily agree with my beliefs and there are some of you who are spiritually awakened but living in the psychic closet facing fears of being accepted. I will impart some words of wisdom. Do what you feel is true to you and for your higher self. Don't worry about what others think of you because someone will always have an opinion of you. I would also say to you that regardless of what life throws at you to always let your light shine and be proud of who you are. Be proud of all the pain you have endured and happiness because it has been the perfect balance that has brought you to the place you are at right now in life. If your church or family condemns you there will always be someone who embraces you and loves you. You are NEVER alone and more importantly don't let anyone mold you for their purposes. You are unique and special and if someone cannot acknowledge this then they are not serving your higher purpose. Lastly, when I said you are not alone I meant it. Take a look all around you, each day there is a new soul being born who is a starseed. You have the indigo children, crystal children and rainbow children. You have the lightworkers, the healers, the psychics, the mediums and the shamans. Everyday someone's light is being awakened and they are stepping into their purpose to make this world a better place in their own unique way. We were born this way! This is our purpose and we are all children of GOD, whether you accept it or not.

Chapter 22

WAKING UP DURING ODD TIMES

We are all focused on time and try to measure our life here in the physical world with the use of time. However, the spiritual world and spirit do not go by earthly time and our own bodies are spiritual souls in a physical body so our bodies will respond accordingly to the amount of spirit around us and the things occurring in our daily lives. It is quite interesting when you notice that there may be days or weeks and you wake up around the same time every single day. Then suddenly it gradually dissipates and you return to a more normal sleeping cycle. I will give a more spiritual explanation for the reason why this could be occurring to you.

Waking up between 9pm – 11pm

This is the time some people try to go to sleep and if you are waking up during this time or finding it very hard to sleep this is going to be dealing more with your right side of the brain and how it deals with creativity, artistic pursuits and intuition. If you are going through a spiritual awakening or noticing, you are trying to tap more into your intuitive side you may notice you have trouble laying down and sleeping during these times or you wake up suddenly around this time. Some psychic and mediums will notice as well that they may have trouble sleeping during these times because spirit usually is more prevalent or known to a mind that is relaxing and not worried by daily pressures. So, if you are very relaxed this is an optimal time for spirit to come around and get your attention. Along with this comes the sleepless moments. While you may be more relaxed spirit could be trying to get your attention, and keeping you awake. Try to pray before laying down and talk to your angels and guides. Ask them to please respect your space and let spirit know that they are not allowed to come through to deliver messages. This is your time to get rest, however, some of us may like this and are not bothered by the activity. To each their own.

Waking up between 12am – 3am

Most people should be asleep during these hours unless you are a night owl or you work nights (graveyard shifts). If you are finding you go to sleep earlier than this time frame and wake up during these hours and must stay awake for a few minutes or longer then you are possibly facing issues within your higher self and the situations occurring in your life. You may be dealing with a hard situation that has affected your ability to trust the universe or the outcome of a situation. You may have repressed emotions that are now playing mind games with you and you cannot let this go easily. There could be an inner war occurring between your higher self (consciousness) and your self-limiting thoughts. You might be seeing something through social conditioning or making a decision based on what you know to be true here in the physical world. One of the ways to work through this is acknowledging and accepting help from the universe and trusting your consciousness. Expressing or showing more self-love to yourself can help you overcome this inner battle of the mind and get some rest. You can also use mantras, meditation, and yoga as other techniques to help you. Some may find that crystals like rose quartz, selenite, and hematite by your bed can help ensure you stay asleep during these hours. Spirit is also very active during these times as well and this is optimal time for dreams to occur that wake you up or you waking up.

Waking up between 3am – 5am

If you are waking up during these times you could be experiencing spiritual activity but you may also find that there are decisions, you are struggling with and this energy has built up and now waking you up during this time. You could also be in a relationship that has your stressed out or there has been something that has affected your love life. Some frustration here that is causing you to wake up specifically during this time. You may feel neglected by others or not as loved and you may also have fear of rejection. If you experienced some form of abuse in your life, you may find that some people will wake up during these time periods as well. The soul recognizes anything that hasn't healed. If you are waking up during these time frames you may need to seek out a reiki master, therapist, or spiritual advisor for some healing and help you achieve the closure you are seeking. You can try using essential oils before going to sleep to help with this. Also, dealing with the problems head on and being vocal on your feelings could help you stop this from occurring.

There are numerous scientific explanations concerning the meridians and ancient Chinese medicine, however, these explanations are more based on spiritual experiences and intuitive guidance from angels and spirit. The explanations here do not and should not take the place of any medical advice from your physician. Use best judgment and try different things that help you to stay asleep during these time frames. As you grow spiritually and go through your spiritual awakenings your mind and soul fuse together and eventually these hours may or may not bother you any longer. Some people are more nocturnal and love and find this time is great for spiritual work and all things dealing with creativity.

Chapter 23

CLAIRALIENCE – THE PSYCHIC SMELL

Often we speak about the other clairs (clairvoyance, claircognizance, clairsentient, and clairaudience) but we rarely speak of the clairalience. This is the sense of being able to smell energy. When you are spiritually awakened or born with these gifts you often have moments where you may at a certain location and pick up on certain fragrances and not even be sure what you are smelling. This could be random and take you by surprise. We often try to find another explanation which could be more scientific and think that our smell is affected by our environment but the truth is spirit is in our environment wherever we are and they can affect our own environment leading to clairalience or as some call it clairessence.

I remember throughout my life there have been so many instances where I have been focusing my energy on one thing such as watching a movie and all sudden I am smelling nachos or some strong cologne but no one is around me. I have walked into a room at other times and smelled chocolate chip cookies. Sure, some might think that we draw these scents out of our own hunger pains or that we have possibly seen these certain items in the last couple of hours and they are now programmed or etched in our memory faculties but the truth is that this isn't the case. It wasn't until I understood that when there is no more logical explanation for such occurrences, it is spirit working this. Being a psychic and medium spirit will use scents to identify them or something that perhaps they used, ate, or were surrounded by to get their energy signature clear. This is a form of spirit communication. The ability for them to use energy and convert that into a scent for us to smell is spirit communication.

I can't tell you how many times I have been asked "How will I know when spirit is around?" If you are picking up on scents this your clairalience picking up on spirit and this is a form of spirit visitation. They are making their presence known through their scent. Some scents will be pleasant and some may be foul smelling. If there isn't a connection with the spirit, you might start smelling other smells. Every soul even living ones have a certain scent that we cannot smell ourselves. However, pets are very intuitive and they know and can pick up our scents. I'm not talking about our smoke scent, or even perfume or colognes. We all have a unique energy signature that emits a scent. Hence this is how our pets know how we are feeling. In many hospice situations when a person who is terminally ill is dying their pet may be able to know and will smell their energy.

What is interesting is how these scents smell coming from a living or spirit. How we vibrate in life will be our energy scent when we pass. Let's say you were someone who always found joy, always was happy, and overall lived a successful life and had no regrets. You will tend to have a sweeter or more appealing scent. Where someone who was a murderer, angry, violent, lied, or even hated would have a putrid smelling scent. This could be like the scent of decay or rot. So, it's safe to say that while we can camouflage certain scents of our physical body our spiritual body itself has a scent.

If you have been smelling different scents and cannot pin point the exact source, write it down and keep a journal of any odd occurrences to refer to. Some things will suddenly make sense after they occur or months later.

Chapter 24

Lessons within a Soul Family

There are so many different reasons why our soul's experience the lessons that we experience here in the physical world. Some of these lessons are to help us grow spiritually and deal with karmic patterns from other past life's we've had. One of the things that my spirit guides have revealed to me as well is that sometimes the way we choose to pass, the hardships we endure, and the joy we share are all intermingled and have connections to our current life and are lessons cause lessons for those in your soul family to learn. I'll repeat it one more time. Our lessons create lessons for those in our soul family.

I'll give you an example, Bobby passed at age 23 and he had his whole life in front of him. His passing was due to driving while under the influence. From his passing his younger brother who looked up to him, learned the effects that alcohol has on the body and what it can cause. His parents knew Bobby had this ongoing addiction to alcohol but could not stop him. This led to the lesson of guilt for his parents as they believe they could have done more to stop this from occurring but the fact is that this was all destined and written to occur. Everyone who Bobby was a part of has been affected by his loss and there are so many possible scenarios. Another scenario would be that Bobby's parents were emotionally void and built up some strong resentment for each other while Bobby was alive. With the passing of Bobby, they felt emotions for the first time and something was stirred up.

Now the same thing also applies to relationships, divorces, and breakups. They all cause us pain and have effects on the children or if there are no children it causes pain we must deal with and we learn from what went wrong in that specific relationship with the hopes of not ever repeating this again. Literally these lessons for our soul are intricate and it could be that a close friend of yours is going to go through the same thing you went through in their relationship and you had to go through the lesson to prepare your soul to help that person with their situation. As you can see our lessons are not stumbling blocks but building blocks for the soul and its greater purpose.

The lessons you learn today will impact you and your soul and give you knowledge and strength you need to overcome the hurdles in life. We often get so frustrated and we don't immediately understand why these things in our life happen such as financial struggles, love struggles, and loss struggles. However, every struggle is a blessing in disguise and there are doors that open from this. Doors to our heart and soul that open lead to more opportunities to help ourselves and others. So, if you are going through some lessons right now that are really difficult know that every lesson will pass and new ones will come in. Some lessons are not painful and spread joy and love and have nothing to do with loss.

Sometimes our hearts must break open for love and light to walk through. It's a transformation we all go through and if you go back to your life and remember all the lessons you have gone through up until this point and think who else was impacted in your family or friends list, you will understand better how this all works. It's not as confusing as it may seem but spirit operates in this manner. Many times, our guides and angels cannot intervene with these lessons and allow them to happen as destiny has it because we would not be the same people we are today, had it not been for going through these lessons.

Chapter 25

VEGANISM AND SPIRITUALITY

There have been a lot of questions asked to me by clients and friends in general in the spiritual community and there is a stigma with meat eaters not being spiritual, so I wanted to take this opportunity to shed some perspective from what I know from my spirits, angels, etc.

First thing let me start off by saying this and that is that deciding to be a vegan or eating meat does not make you any better than anyone else. You are not less spiritual because you eat meat. I have been in contact with several vegans over the years and while most vegans are some of the most gentle and caring people in this world, I have had some encounters where I have been condemned and my spirituality has been questioned because of my choice to eat meat. Yes, I eat meat but while I do, I also eat veggies which I do love as well. Everything in my life is a balance and I do not choose to eat meat every single day. There are days I do fast as well, mainly water or some veggies.

Raymond Guzman

So, if you are a person who eats meat and has been condemned or called unspiritual just ignore the stigma and judgment from others. Eating meat has ancient origins dating back to Indians, Egyptians and some Mesopotamian and other cultures. While I do believe, life is very important some negate the fact that eating plants you are also taking the life of something that was once alive because last time I checked all plants are living as well. In the food chain, most animals who are not omnivores (herb or plant eaters) eat other animals for survival. While we judge other humans for eating meat, we do not judge animals by the same token. This is not meant to poke fun to vegans or meat eaters but stating mere facts.

The main question and issue vegans may have with meat eaters is animal cruelty and the method that some of these slaughter houses have chosen to end the life of an animal for consumption by YOU the consumers. Some have posted videos of how these animals are slaughtered. Some of this may be considered gruesome and to others it may be deemed survival. Most slaughter houses do have laws they must follow and most use methods that are quick to not cause the animal from suffering. While this doesn't make it better, there are many pets and animals who are not slaughtered. Cats, Dogs, Various Birds, wild life and sea food. I don't judge anyone who chooses to follow a vegan path or chooses to eat meat. I do this because I would be living in an ego trap if I judged a vegan who chose to eat meat.

Another topic from some vegans is that with eating meat you are taking into your body the energy of the animal who suffered death in a cruel manner. Again, this could go two ways even with veggies and trees being killed off. Let me explain something, what I do and many spiritual people do is to bless their food. Anything that has energy imprinted on it or was living can have energy cleared and blessed. Before eating any meal, I always say a prayer over my food to take in the sustenance my body needs and to remove all negative energy. It's like healing over your own food, sort of like you would do reiki with another human being. You have that power!

I have been called spiritually unawake or asleep and many others because we choose to eat meat, however, I don't believe spirituality can be defined by what we con-sume but rather your heart and your actions. Some of claimed being vegan or following that diet will enhance, strengthen, or develop your spiritual abilities further, however, some of us are natural born intuitive, mediums, psychics, and healers. Most of us have eaten meat since birth and our abilities are there and very present even with this. Everything we do or eat should be in a healthy balance and there is no negating that eating veggies can help you detox your body, have several healthy benefits, but eating meat occasionally would not hurt you. The fact is that we will continue to see more people follow the vegan or vegetarian path and you will always have meat eaters. I will pray for every living thing on earth and main-tain my inner peace. I am grateful for even having food to eat regardless of it be pure veggies or meat.

Please do not condemn others in the spiritual com-munity or make them feel like they are not spiritual due to their tendencies because you will fall into the ego trap. Judging another is living in their ego. Remember you can bless your food and remove any negative energies attached to it. I hope this information has proven helpful for some of you.

Chapter 26

LOWER LEVEL ENTITIES

We hear this term Lower Level entity often used but what is that exactly. What do we mean? This is a term for a spirit or entity that does not vibrate in the higher levels of earth. These could be people who lived very dark life's while alive and hurt others. These can include murderers, rapists, racists, and much more. Everyone who is alive or in spirit carry energy. Higher level energy is full of feelings of good health, love, smiles, light, warmth, joy, and everything that reminds you of good and happiness. When a person passes, some are earthbound and do not cross over into the light even after having their life review because they fear judgment. They may have done things in this earth they weren't proud of or they may have unfinished business. Some of these that were angry or hateful while alive will carry this energy with them into death. If they are stuck they can be mischievous or harmful. These are the entities that usually do hauntings, cause physical harm, try to scare you and maybe even worse.

How do you discern a lower level entity? Below are some characteristics

- You may feel sick in the presence of a lower level being

- You may smell sulfur or a rotten smell of decay

- You may find that you are scratched, if it is in the set of 3 marks then you are dealing with something demonic.

- You could find that you wake up and feel like your pinned down in bed and cannot move and see others hovering around you. This may or may not be sleep paralysis.

- You could find that things are breaking constantly, people in the house turn against each other constantly for unexplained or petty reasons.

- Certain members or one person in the family has taken on a darker energy that mimics the entity present. So, for example, if the entity was into using black magic, the person may start taking interests into doing black magic or practicing it.

- Suicide- Not all suicides are done by attachments or lower level entities but they can influence some and keep putting the thoughts into their heads.

- You could find nightmares usually involving darker theme can become a nightly occurrence.

- Pets are affected and may whimper or run out of a room as if they fear a certain space.

- Electricity can be affected usually lights will flicker or maybe just an unexplained outage will occur.

- Objects will levitate or move in your presence or out of it.

- Things fly off shelves or tables and break.

- Other sensitive family members or friends come over and feel uncomfortable and feel as if they must leave immediately. Sensitives will feel it the moment they walk into a space that there is something darker or sinister.

- If you find you do have something darker the lower level entity could possibly be demonic but in all cases, it may be just a darker spirit who refuses to leave.

There are several things you can do to rid yourself of it but you must remember not every situation will apply to you depending on how many are present, the land itself, the history of the land or house, etc.

Here are some ways to protect yourself and your space.

- Ask the soul to leave and cross in the light. Some may not realize they are dead and need to be told forcibly to leave.

- Sage, Palo Santo, and Frankincense should be burned in every room of the house, not in just in the room that activity is most present because once you cleanse that room what do you think the spirit will do? It will go to the other rooms so every room must be done and while burning this try to go through all 4 corners of every room and doorways and windows and ask all negative spirits to leave and only love and light can stay. I recommend all windows and doors being opened while you do this to allow the spirit to exit.

- Open windows and clean clutter. A dusty place or place filled of many objects that belonged to others is a magnet for spirit activity and sometimes intelligent spirits can hide in these objects. Remember to sage or cleanse anything that is used and given to you or that you buy.

- Place religious or sacred objects like crosses, crucifixes, Hamsa, Star of David, Buddha in every space.

- Sprinkle holy water or anointed oil around the house especially on windows or doorways. Again, depending on your belief system.

- Prayer is essential and if you are more spiritual than religious you can say prayers of your choice to invite your angels to protect you and bring light into your space.

- You can also use protective crystals and place them in each corner of every room of your house to create like a crystal grid or barrier/shield.

If all of this fails and you feel you are dealing with something you don't know how to handle, be sure to seek out a medium or paranormal investigation team for guidance and they may be able to do further investigation to get down to the bottom of it.

Whatever you are going through, it is important for families who are haunted to reunite in one room until a paranormal investigator or medium can help you. Family that sticks together is stronger than one person. A lower level entity can be so smart they will prefer each family member to be separated to target one person at a time and weaken them. They feed off fear, because fear is like a buffet of food for them. They will get stronger and know your weakness. NEVER fear, only have LOVE and HOPE in your heart and soul. Do not communicate with it or threaten it as it could make matters worse.

In most cases these entities can be crossed over or just removed forcibly through a home blessing or through a medium acting as an intercessor or pathway for the soul to communicate with. If it is something more sinister and malevolent sometimes the house itself or land may have to go through an extreme situation which may merit an exorcism of the house itself.

Remember that your guardian angels are always protecting you and if you find that you are living with a lower level entity in most cases a passed loved one will be there also protecting and guiding you so you are NOT alone. I hope this helps you get a better understanding on what a lower level entity is and thank you again.

Chapter 27

TWIN FLAMES/SOULMATES THE ERA OF COMPLICATED RELATIONSHIPS

This has been something that someone during a live session brought up and while I did cover this, I wanted to take some time to discuss why we are seeing so many disruptions around love when love is supposed to be forever. While love is forever and has always existed both in the spiritual realm and earth, right now on earth we are seeing a lot of these soulmate and twin flame relationships going south. There is a lot of temptation, unions that provide healing, and some that last a lifetime.

The real question is why now? So, let me explain, we are all living in different level or states of consciousness. You can have someone who is living in the third dimension of consciousness. This type of person is still stuck in old thought patterns, temptations and lust are very strong and in most cases these people will cheat on their partners, lie, and hurt them spiritually and emotionally. The impact of this is very severe especially if the other partner who is the victim is already living in the fourth or fifth dimension. The world is currently operating on a fifth dimension of consciousness.

This is a very evolved state in which there are more AWAKENED folks who are now aware of the bigger picture or their higher self. Those who are living in this dimension or state of consciousness are very aware of healing the world needs and will value their connections and relationships. There is a high level of loyalty, they will leave negativity of any kind behind. This includes relationships where they have tried to bring their partner to another state of consciousness and awareness. They do not tend to give up on their relationships easily and do not see failure as an option. They will try everything from traditional methods to untraditional like counseling, psychology, discussing, giving second chances, forgiving, reiki, crystal healing, magic, and the list goes on and on. However, once all options are exhausted a person living in the fifth dimension knows that their soul cannot continue to operate from a place of pain and will not continue to try to change someone who is still living in the third dimension. Therefore, a lot of people are separating more now than ever, or finding their partners struggle with communication and accepting their higher self.

A person still living in the third level of consciousness is not going to be able to discuss things more openly and will keep fighting their partners who are living in the fifth dimension. So, what keeps two people together even if they are on different levels of consciousness/dimensions? The answer to this is your free will. This is a higher power that you were given to govern your own life and co-create your reality that you wish to have here on earth.

What many do not realize is that while someone who is still stuck in the third or fourth dimensions can be helped to be brought into a higher state of conscious-ness. You are not doomed to continue to live in this. Many of these souls have not been able to ascend into these higher levels or had a spiritual awakening because they do not understand what they are going through and just know what they are immediately feeling spiritually. If you are stuck in a relationship and you are living in a higher level of consciousness you can help your partner and I will list some ways. If you are both living in the third or fourth dimension these methods I provide below will also assist you to get to a higher state of consciousness.

Methods to ascending into a higher state of con-sciousness:

MEDITATION - Meditation is key and there is no right way or wrong way. Your eyes don't have to be closed, they can be open. You just need to spend either 10-15 minutes practicing being alone and spending time alone with only yourself. Stare blankly at an object far away and keep your vision on it and just continue to breath. In your mind ask your guides and ascended masters to help you. You don't need to mention any specific names or chant. Spirit is very aware. If you prefer closing your eyes, close your eyes and breathe and don't think about anything going on in your life, just focus on the darkness or light you see. Do the same thing by asking your guides and ascended masters to step forth and help guide you. You might not see anything and think you are crazy. LOL Yes, it can be rather hilarious but with any technique it does require practice and practice does make perfect. Keep doing this and you can modify how many times you do this a week.

The more awakened you are, the less meditation you will require per week. Three to four times a week in the beginning will help you.

DEAL WITH YOUR FEELINGS – Many of us cannot enter a new phase in our spiritual path because we are still clinging to past hurt. This could have been sexual, physical, or emotional abuse we endured in our life. This affects our souls. It's easier to bury these feelings and not acknowledge that we haven't dealt with them. This often, creates stagnation at the soul level and instead of being able to move forward, you are doing yourself a disservice and creating blocks. So regardless of anything positive that is happening in your life, you will always be pessimistic or negative towards the blessings unfolding before you. You will also notice you fear change, you have a certain outlook on life and expect that all people will judge you or have the same behavior of those who hurt you. Dealing with your feelings is not easy, it's not something that you can fix in a week or month. Slowly, you need to open to someone you trust. If you feel you can't open up to others, then just speak out loud or in your inner mind to your angels. It will be your own voice chit chatting with yourself because you might not hear your angels talking back to you or interacting with you. It's okay. The hardest part is opening up to someone else but the moment you do, your soul will feel uplifted and you will feel lighter. The worst thing you can do, is to live with that spiritual congestion in your soul. By speaking about it and acknowledging you are no longer that person in the past and you are not afraid, you are dealing with the issues that are holding you back. Slowly as you let go of these past hurts, you will notice your intuition becomes stronger and that you are entering a new era spiritually. This is stepping into a new state of consciousness, you are now aware that these old thought patterns are no longer who you are, and they do not serve a greater purpose.

REIKI/PAST LIFE REGRESSION – These are spiritual tools that you can seek out and reiki focuses on energy healing at the spiritual level and releasing areas of those energy points in your body that are still blocked. This can be very effective to helping you achieve a greater sense and awakening. Some will also seek out past life regression and this is like therapy in the sense you deal with past life issues that have followed you into this current life you're living now. You will be surprised how many of us still have past life fears, karmic issues that have followed us and hold us back. By going back in time and understanding your past life, you can benefit and re-lease these blocks as well.

DOING WHAT YOU WANT – So many of us want to make our parents happy or live their dream for our perfect life. When this happens, we are not able to live our life on our own terms as it was intended to be lived. Many of us go into careers just because of the money or title thinking that it will bring us happiness but deep down you will feel unhappy and in most cases money cannot buy happiness. Therefore, at first it may be sunshine and like a honeymoon but after a few years in one career or profession many find stagnation or that these positions no longer satisfy them. It feels redundant and draining. The greatest purpose you can have here on earth is to work in a profession that brings you the most happiness and joy. If it doesn't feel like a job and more like something you wake up and look forward to doing, then this is you experiencing your soul shifting and expanding. You will be entering a new level of consciousness. When you do what you want, you will find that money is also not a factor because spiritually you are guided and will find ways to expand your earnings or expand your business. A lot of our financial worries are centered around us not being in a job or position that truly makes us feel whole. Do what you want and what makes you happy. Don't worry about what others think of you. Even if it's a spiritual path, it will be rewarding. You don't earn brownie points but you do earn angel wings. See, the work you are doing here on earth is far greater to your soul's evolution and helps you move forward. Some of you may be reading this and thinking how does this possibly affect a relationship and what does it have to do with the third or fifth dimension? It has a lot of impact because re-lationships often revolve around financial struggles and which partner is bringing in the most money or who has more financial independence.

As you can see there are many shifts occurring in the world right now and it's a joyous time to be living here in the physical world and living with your soulmate or twin flame and being in a state of awareness is momentous. If you are living in the fourth or fifth dimension kudos to you. If you are living in the third dimension do not give up hope, either you yourself are slowly moving towards that greater consciousness or your partner will try everything in their power to help you. It won't be easy but you can do it. Value your relationships, know that no relationship is truly perfect even if you are living in a more evolved state of consciousness you will always find that there is going to be disagreements or arguments but they only make your relationship stronger because of the love you have is stronger than anything else. Hold onto LOVE like it is the life force you breathe.

Chapter 28

Transitioning Process: Last Words Spoken

The topic of death sometimes scares us. It's because we have become so comfortable in this body and the world that we are in and have created bonds and family in this reality, that we begin to forget this truly isn't home. This is a temporary space which we occupy filled with lessons, journeys, and spiritual growth. Once we are done here we will transition out of this body which is the vessel that holds the soul and ascend to the spiritual realm. The spiritual realm is often referred to the afterlife, heaven, dimensions, but regardless of the word we use, it's HOME!

This is a reality that exists where all souls exist and within this space we are all connected on one vibration of love and the divine source aka GOD exists there. GOD isn't a person, but spirit often referred to as the Consciousness. He is the master spirit as I would like to refer to him and is pure loving energy. In this space many of us live in that space. However, there are many hierarchies within this spiritual realm. Like a pyramid the lower levels are places where souls who had a lower vibration will go to and spend some time there to be helped by angels and guides to see their errors, their opportunities, and what else they need to do to ascend to the higher levels. They are not stuck there. I already probably have some of your asking a lot more questions and some may be confused, but that's okay.

I will get back on track and explain what happens to our souls when we are transition and the days, weeks, months, hours before passing. Now many of you have been with your loved ones right before they passed and heard them mumble things you could not interpret or comprehend. Were they hallucinating? No! Could they be really medicated and having unexplained conversations with themselves? No! But you clearly hear them carrying on conversations. But with who? In most cases, these conversations are taking place telepathically between their soul and visitors. These visitors are passed loved ones who have come to prepare the soul and take them with them, passed loved ones giving a message, guides, and angels. Since some people are in comas, had a stroke, or more a part of their brain function is limited but their soul is fully aware of their surroundings, what you're saying, what is going on here in the physical world and in the spiritual world. Since they are incapacitated in some way physically in their body and their soul is trying to communicate telepathically, the physical body still wants to say something but is unable to say certain things clearly or if they can utter complete words or partial sentences, it may not make sense to you. But trust me, they are carrying on conversations with the other side.

I often get asked, if our loved one is carrying on conversations with our passed grandma or other family members should this be our sign that their soul is getting ready to depart from this reality or they are getting ready to die? NO! Like I said, not every instance or circumstance is going to be the same and this doesn't mean they are going to likely pass away. Many people have often confused this as a true sign of someone getting ready to pass. While this is still true in many cases for souls who are getting ready to depart, some are just being comforted and given messages from their loved ones, that they may or may not remember when they wake up or in a conscious state.

For those souls who are being helped to transition over, their loved one, an angel, guide, or someone else in their spiritual family may be there and extend their hand to cross them over or they might see a bright light to go through. This would be the portal or opening to the spiritual realm. Some souls may have unfinished business here in the physical world and decide to stay earthbound so they will not cross. Some may be aware of their passing or how they passed and some may be clueless that they are dead. However, after some time, they do get some assistance from the spiritual side and given a choice to stay here or cross over.

Again, I will stress that those who have suffered a stroke, in a coma whether medically induced or otherwise, their soul is aware of everything going on. When they wake up, some may remember some may not. Those who don't remember anything have chosen to not remember because it wasn't necessary. Those that do remember, usually have important messages for their existing loved ones and themselves. They remember because they were given information to change or alter their life path or soul path.

If you are a medium or psychic with telepathic or clairaudient abilities, you could easily tune into your loved one's soul who is getting ready to transition and many times, they are communicating with us days or hours before they are ready to pass. You will hear them usually say, it's me....don't worry....I'm here with you! Often, we think it's our own voice we hear in the mind and while that is sometimes the case, that voice of yours is spirit speaking through you. Their soul and your soul have tuned into the same frequency and you are able to hear them clearly in your mind like a radio station or television playing. So don't discount this as just it being your imagination. I could go on and on about different experiences but know that those loved ones who are transitioning are okay. It's always our physical body that feels pain on a physical and emotional level but our soul is perfection. In our soul, we feel no pain. Be sure to express how much you love those around you while they can communicate with you because many of us go through life with regrets of not being able to say goodbye or understand the last words spoken. When we have expressed our love, even if we don't get to say goodbye, our soul knows that love is a universal language in which no barriers exist.

Chapter 29

SPIRIT LED – LISTENING TO SPIRIT

When we hear the words led by Spirit it's hard to imagine a spiritual being pulling your hand or pushing you in a certain direction. However, you would be so surprised to realize how much work your guides, angels and spiritual guidance team is doing from the background. What does it feel like and how do you know the difference between being led by spirit or something else?

The first thing to know is that there is no certain guidelines and your spirits are tailored to your specific needs and they are able to guide you by putting ideas in your head, giving you this unexplained feeling to go forward, putting signs or symbol directly in your path, through dreams, through meditation, through prayer and the list goes on and on. The key here is that spirit has no boundaries when they are ready to lead you but you must be ready to lead you.

The thing I found most interesting through my own experiences is that when I cast my fears aside and just trusted the universe the most miraculous opportunities and assistance was readily available. Sometimes this in the form of a good friendship, long conversations, a favor, or a selfless act. Other times it could be in the form of a lucky windfall or abundance that comes to you. When I was able to let go of any self-doubt and thinking too far out in the future, I noticed that I was able immediately live in the present. Enjoying the present moment is part of being led by spirit. The other side has nothing but time to spare, we here on earth are the ones who are too fixated on deadlines, getting something done by a certain date and work around a system used to measure time. With work, errands, family and more the human mind often cannot separate or differentiate the difference between the present and what's to come.

Spirit will not always talk to you but they will guide you where you need to go, and a part of your soul can listen or choose to ignore it. This is where your free will comes into play. Spirit has certain limitations and cannot intervene in your free will. However, if you are open to working with spirit and allowing them to guide you they will choose an easier path for you, than you would chose for yourself. Your choices sometimes are full of obstacles, roadblocks, setbacks...well you get the picture by now. Sometimes being led by spirit will bypass these things and still allow you to see the outcome of a poor choice indirectly or directly. You could see a best friend going through a situation that you would be in if you had made their choices and this is what I mean when I say that you sometimes see the bigger picture and how wonderful it is to be led by spirit.

To be led by spirit you must first raise your vibration. You might be asking what does that even mean? It just means living in authenticity, not judging others, loving one another and yourself, listening to your intuition, trusting the universe. These things bring balance and harmony and angels and spirit guides vibrate on those levels as well. So, it's no surprise that they would be able to lead you where you need to go. Now if you are vibrating low and full of the opposite feelings and emotions described above, then you will most likely find it harder to be led by spirit. This is where ego steps in and sometimes we allow negative energy to pervade and guide us. This is often met with disappointment, setbacks, heartache, anger, resentment etc.

Allowing spirit to be part of our lives is such a privilege and honor. You will learn to trust yourself more and to trust your spiritual guidance team and know that any recommendations they make to you or put in your head is really for your greater good. Listen and trust what you feel because those feelings that seem minor are the greatest voices of spirit that should be listened to. Love yourself and love as much as you can and the connection between you and spirit will become inseparable.

Chapter 30

ARE YOU A NATURAL BORN WITCH?

People can identify themselves as witches because they either practice witchcraft or can identify themselves as either pagan or wiccan. However, how do you distinguish someone who was innately born with mystical powers or abilities? This chapter will be providing you with a list of characteristics that can help you determine the possibility you were born a natural witch.

Many also believe that the term witch relates to just a female but what do you call a male who was born a natural witch? The answer would be that there is no specific gender to be called a witch so the term can be used synonymously for both females and males.

Here's a list of characteristics that you may display if you were born a natural witch:

- **Night Terrors** – You could have been afraid of the dark as a child. The reason was that either you saw spirit from an early age or new that there were other worldly creatures that exist. However, most adults would dismiss this as an active imagination, most kids who are gifted from a young age know better.

- **Alienation/Isolation** – In elementary and throughout your schooling you may feel different than other kids your age. You might find that in isolation you feel happier and you learn to increase your awareness of the things around you. Able to find comfort in your own power without following the in crowd. Most natural born witches don't crave popularity as they honor their uniqueness.

- **Bullying** – Most natural born witches experience some form of bullying through their childhood and even adulthood. Others who fear you, manifest their fear as anger or hatred. Those who burned your ancestors or come from a family that burned your ancestors who were fellow witches or magical may have reincarnated into this life time and their soul still remembers your power. Most bullies feel your power and bully you because they know you are special.

- **Affinity to Black Clothing** – As cliché as this sounds, yes it's true any witch can wear other colors other than black, but most witches find black as powerful. It can absorb negative energy and then dispel it. Black is not only slimming and a universal color but it's magically powerful. Some prefer getting their toe nails or finger nails painted black as well.

- **Cats** – You may notice your favorite animal is a cat. However, you most likely love all animals, but you find cats are attracted to you and find your energy calm and soothing. They most likely gravitate towards you. Other pets may feel very alert when you walk into a room and may be quiet.

- **Moles/Birth Marks** – Many natural born witches have beauty marks that may have been passed down from their ancestors through each generation. This helps them identify their ancestry down each generation.

- **Magical Abilities** – Since a child you may have thought of something happening and it happened. Often natural born witches can will things into existence. This is different as manifesting be-cause it occurs much faster than something that manifests.

- **Moon** – Find out what moon you were born under by pulling up your birth chart. Depending on what moon you were born under, that time during the month may be a peak time for you and your magical abilities. Senses and abilities like your intuition, spell casting, and more are more powerful during this time.

- **Palm Markings** – It is believed that most who have a cross or several on their palms are mark-ings of those who had past life's as witches and were burned at the stake. It's like the ultimate sacrifice and these markings also signify you have great power and will accomplish what you came to earth to do. Your path is often a more difficult one in all areas but especially love and relationships.

- **Piercing Eyes** – Natural born witches often have a strong or penetrating gaze that others notice or look away. You may get told often that there is something about your soul and eyes that are special. You seem to be able to see beyond this world and into the soul of others. Most who possess psychic abilities often can be identified as natural born witches or at least identify with more than five in the list.

- **Apple Juice** – This one may have you rolling your eyes but after what I tell you, you may not think this is so crazy. If you are a natural born witch you may prefer apples than oranges or orange juice. The reason is that when you cut an apple in half, the seeds form a pentagram or pentacle which is a very powerful source of energy. Ancients would cut apples and throw them around their property for protection from harm or evil.

- **Unexplained Obsession** – As a natural born witch you may have been fascinated in all areas of the occult of spiritual such as vampirism, witchcraft, magic, faeries, herbs, healing, and the list goes on and on. You may not be able to explain why but you felt drawn to these things and you may have felt that it was familiar to you or felt like you have done this before. Many natural born witches will purchase a tarot deck and practice at a young age without knowing why. It's the calling of a witch. Being a natural your soul is remembering things from previous lives.

- **Green Thumb** – You may feel very connected to mother nature and trees specifically. Outdoors you feel more alive and you may prefer to walk barefoot rather than with shoes. Your body can easily connect to the earth and you feel as one.

- **Traumatic Life Events** – Usually natural born witches experience at some time in their life a traumatic even that sets them on a different course but also strengthens their abilities. This could be the passing of someone special, a wreck, a health condition or etc. Again, as natural born witches we often have the hardest life paths on earth and our lessons are different but in each lesson your power grows. Think back to a traumatic time period and how you learned from that lesson and now use it to your advantage.

- **Family Issues** – Growing up, you most likely questioned whether you were from the same family or adopted. You could have always felt like your family didn't love you or appreciate you or you could have felt like they were your family. Natural born witches are often very opinionated and hard to influence. They march to the beat of their drum and like to do things their way.

- **Crystals/Creative Arts** – Natural born witches express themselves often through some form of art or crystals. Many use them for healing but also as amulets of protection. Usually you will express yourself through painting, sculpting, jewelry making, and etc.

- **Spiritually Conscious** – Most natural born witches do not like school and find teachings and things in text books as lies and no use for that stuff. Many like to be self-taught and learn things naturally and vibrate at a higher level of consciousness. So, they typically don't follow the masses and stand out. They came to change the world or impact the world in a positive manner. They are not socially conditioned and can discern between worldly lies and the truth.

- **Traveling** – Many natural born witches will want to travel or feel the desire to visit land that is almost calling to them half across the world. Regardless of the distance they will find a way. Energy exists in different areas and some places like the Mayan Ruins, The Stonehenge, are all full of magical power that once a natural born visit can unlock magical power within themselves. These areas are energy points on earth and therefore these structures are still standing. Our ancestors worshipped these areas and found great knowingness and power in them.

Having a greater understanding of your own capabilities and power is amazing. Many may have had feelings they were witches but not aware. Hopefully you could identify with at least 4 – 5 talking points. If you did the chances you are a natural born witch is very high in the scale. Don't be afraid to travel into the unknown, instead embrace it.

Chapter 31

SPIRIT CLOCK VS. EARTHLY CLOCK

Have you ever wondered how a loved one who has passed knew you were going to be in some accident and saved your life? Perhaps there was a life and death situation and your guardian angel were there protecting you. How did they know to be there? Spirit is all around us this is true, but it's a little more complicated than you might think. Perhaps you had a visitation from spirit weeks prior to you going on a paranormal research trip. How does spirit know you are the one appointed to help? How do they know you are a medium perhaps coming to help them cross over? These are all great questions and I will explain this in greater detail.

Recently, I had a conversation with a colleague who is also a friend of mine. She works with holistic medicine and also negative energy removal and is wonderful at her craft. During our conversation she had a gentleman who was earthbound appearing to her days before she had to visit a client's house. She was not sure how he knew she would be coming and why would he be waiting there. This brought us to both discussing this topic further.

You see once we pass into the spiritual realm it doesn't matter if our soul is earthbound or has already crossed over to the other side. Once our physical body dies that earthly time we are governed by which is a 24 hr cycle stops to exist and matter to us. Our souls and spirit don't operate on that time. In fact, their time is very accelerated. This explains how spirit knows things that are coming up or that will come to pass. How can they know. It's like a movie to them playing on the other side. They are very aware of our destinies and path and while we live out of lives, they will be there to help guide and protect us. Now they cannot interfere with our exit points, meaning we all choose a certain time our soul will leave the physical earth. However, if we are in danger, our loved ones will step in or our guardian angels and they know.

If they have an important message and you are the person destined to help cross them over or relay the message to a living person, they can appear in your home, in your dreams, weeks or days before you relay the message. They recognize your energy and probably have seen it already on the other side. Think of this reality as a tv show to spirit. Each person has their own show and spirit watches our episodes. Quite funny right? But it makes sense the more you think of it.

Earthbound spirits also pick up on an energy of a medium or channeler and regardless of where you are, they see a light almost like a halo surrounding your body. They know who can see and help them or hear them. You cannot hide this from them. This is why you may be somewhere random and get multiple spirits coming through or even being in a large crowd and spirit coming to you. The strongest souls will come through.

Going back on subject, when people have a Near Death Experience (NDE) they often lose track of time and when they return to their physical body, they usually say it felt like they were on the other side for months or years. It's because our soul frequency is already programmed for earth and when we step into the spirit world, our true frequency and time is activated.

Chapter 32

Pets and the Afterlife

It is important to know that our fur babies are with us in spirit after they pass. Ever heard that saying that all dog's souls go to heaven? Well it's true but it's all animals. Their souls are unique and usually they come here to earth to be our companions and help heal us. They also are very intuitive. They serve many purposes. As a psychic medium I often do pet readings and I find such great joy doing mediumship readings for animals that have passed. Your pets do often visit just like souls of humans do when they cross over.

Many of you may have had your own personal experiences where other pets in the family start barking into a blind space. To your eyes, you may not see anything there but if spirit of another pet that's crossed is there, most animals will see them. They could also feel them. The hardest thing to do is often let go of our pets when they are sick. I recently had an experience in which a friend who had a fur baby, noticed a change in the behavior of their puppy. In many cases when your pet is ready to cross over willingly and without intervention or assistance, you could notice that they may lose appetite, they lack interest in the usual.

Many just lay there without energy. They could be sleeping more than normal just like a human soul that passes from a terminal illness or an illness that weakens them. One common thing is that the person starts sleeping a lot. This is because the soul of pets are using their remaining energy to transition to the other side. It's hard to see but in several instances, I have witnessed myself that this occurs.

Most people who have a strong bond with their pets may also feel premonitions before they pass. This could be like upset stomach, nausea and feeling impending doom or anxiety. This is because energetically you are linked to your fur baby and their soul is preparing your soul for the acceptance of this. While it's not easy to accept, none of us want to see our pets suffer or be sick. Just like human souls, if your pet had cancer or other illnesses and was in pain, they are healed immediately and not in any pain when they cross over.

Sometimes they will leave you signs before passing and this could be some clumps of their fur, a barking, you could feel like a brush of air on your feet or ankles. If they always sat on your lap or on your bed, you could still feel that pressure or indent. Another common question that is often wondered is that if souls of pets reincarnate just like human souls do? The answer to that is that yes, they can but pets are different in their souls. Since they are pure of heart and come here selflessly to earth to help humanity, they don't have karmic lessons like we do. However, they can come back as your spirit guide, and guardian angel.

Do your fur babies have messages for you once they have passed? Yes, many of them know that their family here do not have closure or may be concerned. It's not uncommon for them to give messages just as human spirits do. Spirit is a soul and it doesn't matter if they never spoke like a human does. The language of the soul is universal. This is a big misconception.

If you have lost your pet, know that their love is unconditional. They appreciate everything you have done. If you didn't get to say goodbye, they know and can hear you from the other side. Many families who lose a pet due to an accident or in a tragic way often have grief thinking that their fur baby didn't get to say good bye or they didn't get to say goodbye. Nothing is left unsaid when you have a special bond with any soul. They see more than you imagine from the other side. They encourage us and still love us. These bonds are unbreakable.

Chapter 33

Signs Angels are Near

I often receive this question and how do you know if your angels are around you? It's important to know that angels are assigned to us at birth and are with us throughout our journey here in the physical world. We also can have more than one angel assigned to us as well. Their mission is to be with us and the only time they may not be able to really protect us, is when we are vibrating at lower levels of energy.

This is because the angels and archangels operate in the light and full of love. In turn, when we operate from love and light our angels can really be present and show us that they are there. When we are vibrating at a lower energy that is full of anger or discord, this is when angels tend to be there but cannot really help us. The reception and protection aren't the best and this is because this isn't the frequency they operate on. Therefore, some people who are very depressed, just experienced a loss, or cannot forgive, usually cannot connect with their angels.

I will go on to say that angels do hear everything you say and communicate to them. It doesn't matter if you say it in your mind or out loud, they know.

So here are some signs that your angels are near:

- You feel a presence that is full of love always watching you or around. It's not scary but rather lovingly.
- You see blue speckles of light, gold, or any other color appear quickly. This can be during meditation or while awake.
- You can see a bright light appear and then disappear.
- You often find feathers around you.
- Every time you are going through something rough you will tend to see butterflies, doves, any kind of bird.
- You see angel numbers frequently like 222, 12:12, 11:11, 333.
- You came close to being hurt in an accident or an accident was prevented.
- You feel a warmth deep within radiating out (the touch of an angel).
- You hear a high-pitched frequency in your ear or ringing.
- You tend to gravitate towards angelic things like angel wings, angel pendants, angel artwork, etc.
- You smell floral fragrances that you have never or rarely smell (gardenia, rose, and etc).
- You tend to find someone following you while out in public and then watching you but they disappear and you never see them again.

- You feel an overwhelming sense of inner stillness and calmness.

These are just a few ways of knowing that you are not alone, and spirit is always around you. You never have to worry with angels that are protected. The will help guide you and when they are present evil cannot be present. Evil usually evades or runs away from the light and from angels. Angels do not require sleep as they are spiritual in nature so they are around us 24/7.

Chapter 34

GEOMETRIC FIGURES & UNIVERSAL DOWNLOADS

How weird is it during your down time you may be laying down with your eyes closed and see odd colorful shapes and symbols? You may be asking yourself what this means to you other than beautiful shapes. Well this is called sacred geometry and can be a full array of intricate patterns, shapes, designs. When one sees these, they can be in meditation, almost at the point right before sleep but consciously awake. You may also see them during a wake state and randomly they appear.

If you are seeing these, chances are that you are very spiritually awakened. This means your consciousness is expanded and very aware of the universe. Nothing is just black and white to you. Your soul is essentially transforming but this still doesn't answer the question as to why you are seeing these. Anyone who is awakened is open to the universe and receiving what we call codes or downloads of information. These figures are messages encoded and may be appearing because the universe is preparing you for something that has happened in your waking life that you need answers too or have been asking for signs. You may not understand by seeing them but your wisdom expands and so you usually see these when your soul is preparing to handle a situation that may require wisdom beyond your years or wisdom that is beyond our physical understanding.

There is nothing to be afraid of although you can also see faces, in addition to the shapes. The faces or images could be visions you are seeing and spirit showing you things, so you can hold onto that information and later use that to help someone else or pass messages to others. After you start releasing the need to understand these and just write what you saw down, or you choose to help another person with your Universal downloads you will notice that you will see these less frequently.

During these episodes of downloads, you may find that you are tired or fatigued. You could notice you are more sensitive to energy. Because these downloads come directly from the universe and spiritual in nature and we are spiritual beings living an earthly experience some of these downloads take time to translate or make sense to our body. Our body is composed of energy and uses our energy to translate and make sense of these things. When you see these symbols or downloads of info be sure to treat yourself with self-love and allow yourself to reprogram.

After this experience you may find that others are more attracted to your energy and come to you searching for answers even if you don't think you are the right person to be asked. Know also if you are experiencing sacred geometry and downloads you will come more strongly into your spiritual gifts shortly afterwards. You could find your intuition is stronger than ever.

The universe always provides what we need and everyone's downloads and symbols will be different and tailored to their specific needs and path.

Chapter 35

DID SOMEONE DIE IN YOUR HOTEL ROOM?

If you are looking for spirits or perhaps just traveling you would be surprised to know that hotels are one of the #1 places that can be full of spirit activity. Why? It's because so many travel yearly to thousands of locations and usually stay in a hotel. Some NEVER make it out alive. Therefore, some are left earthbound.

If someone died in the room due to natural causes or were murdered, chances are the hotel isn't going to let you know that this occurred. After all they are in the business of making money. When a person has been murdered in a hotel room all things like carpet, furniture, mattresses are disposed of. This includes electronic devices like TV because blood can be spattered into the crevices and once turned on the heat can give off a smell of death.

However, there are things that cannot be disposed of only covered up. So, if you are in a hotel where there were gunshots look at the walls. Usually hotels are not going to call in construction crews to patch the holes in the wall and paint over it. They will usually get the maintenance crew on it. If you are staying at a hotel look at all the walls and see if the paint is blotchy or one area seems patched up or uneven. If the ceiling also looks off this could be due to blood splattered or gunshots that made holes.

Another sign is an awful stench of death like rotten smell that does not go away. Often maintenance and cleaning crew only change our air vents occasionally or change the filter once or twice a year. If you are smelling something foul it could be that blood or other body fluids have seeped down into the air condition and emit an order.

If there is no food and flies around the room or around light fixtures this could be due to numerous things. However, when bodies are left in the room and decomposing for days, flies will form and usually cling to the light fixtures.

If the room is partially renovated then chances something awful happened.

During Hurricane Harvey I had the pleasure of staying almost a month and a half in a hotel and while my room did not seem off. When I would lay down on my bed I would feel uncomfortable and could feel energy from the previous people who had laid down before me there in that spot. If you are an empath or sensitive you are going to feel odd if the energy is off. Be sure to carry some protective crystals and if you have a smoking room then take some sage. Use that to clear the energy around the bed and rooms of your hotel suite. I also noticed that the area near the corridor had some negative energy and some rooms on the bottom floor I could feel as I walked past some rooms that there had been domestic violence, arguments, and fights. Usually when you pass a room you will feel either sick, a knot in your stomach, or you can just feel the negative energy. One thing I would do was to sit in the pool area and see the cleaning staff. In some rooms after they came out of them, they were a different energy and mood wise. Some they didn't take long in so I know their moods were not attributed to the room being dirty. Some of the rooms had been vacant but they still have to clean them or get them ready for huge events that will draw tourists to the town and hotel.

Pay attention to strange sounds or cold spots in your hotel room. You could also feel a presence in your room like someone watching you. If you notice temperature changes and there is no ventilation near that area or drafts, it could be spirit around you and occupying that space as well. If you suspect someone passed in your room, you can request another room but have a good reason. It will all depend on vacancies and whether they are willing to do that.

Chapter 36

CAN SPIRITS HARM THE LIVING?

We all have seen a haunted movie or heard that spirits can inflict harm to the living if they are truly angry or upset. Is there any truth to this? You have to understand that just like there are good spirits, there are a lot of bad spirits. These were either dark souls who lived a very dark path while on earth and have chosen to not cross over into the light. These are earthbound spirits. Most earthbound spirits do not cross into the spiritual realm because they either feel scared that they will be judged on the other side when they cross into the light. The other reason is that they want revenge. If they were murdered or died in a tragic manner, they may also be staying behind because they want revenge on the person who is living and did this to them. Sometimes they stay behind after death because they have living loved ones who they feel need them or they need to get a message across to them before they get their peace. Now that I've explained the different types of earthbound spirits, I'm going to focus on the darker energies who can cause harm to the living and how they do this.

Now darker energies or negative spirits have various reasons why they want to cause harm to the living. They either want to send a clear message you are crossing their territory, you've done something to draw their attention, they were mental in life and in death still carry this quality, and in some cases you don't have to do anything... they are just evil and get sick pleasure of torturing human souls.

Now energies such as the ones I'm describing in this chapter can in fact cause different things to occur in your environment and not necessarily cause physical harm. Think of them trying to give you a message that they are present in your home. Most people who have been haunted or live in a haunted house can see the following things occur.

- Lights flicker
- Doors Open and Shut
- Things are misplaced
- Animals are afraid to go into a certain area or bark incessantly at odd hours of the day or night
- Animals are drawn to one area in particular and seem more aggressive but you can't see what they see
- Disembodied voices can be heard
- Apparitions
- Weird Stenches or smells (some are the scent of death...decay and rotten or putrid in smell)
- Scratching or Tapping on the walls

- Phone calls but when you are on the line, the other line there is just static or noise
- Feeling someone is watching you in your home
- Feeling hair pulled
- Feeling someone is touching you
- Feeling someone lying next to you in bed
- Feeling uneasy
- Feeling headaches, nausea, dizzy, some other sickness that appears mysteriously

The list goes on and on.

Now there are some questions if darker energies can cause illnesses or medical conditions and in some cases death. The answer to this is YES. Some of these may be darker energies and some may be what we call demonic. Here is a list of actual things that can happen when they become more physical

- You have dark nightmares, usually someone you love is dying, being killed, but they are still living
- You sometimes notice yourself or your family members in the home seem possessed or besides themselves.
- Sudden or unexplained arguments and outburst of anger
- Scratches appear on your body and burn shortly after appearing or you wake up with them (De-

monic attacks usually result in 3 scratches which look like a set of claws just scratched you. This is to mock the trinity. Again, this will all depend on your spirituality and what religious background you had before becoming spiritual in nature....so your interpretation may vary).

- Waking up with strange bruises
- Feeling sick in a certain room or place.
- Sudden and overwhelming anxiety attacks that seem to intensify in a certain room or only in your home.
- Waking up or feeling pressure on your chest while laying on your bed
- Sleep paralysis

The thing with darker energies and the demonic is that the longer a human person is exposed to this energy and depending on how strong the entity is they can cause or bring about very bad health conditions like heart attacks, irregular heartbeats, strokes, and yes even some cancers. Some of you may be reading this and think this is ridiculous, however, hear me out. I will go on to explain this further.

You see when you have a dark entity, and, in some cases, some people have many in one area or place, they vibrate at very darker levels. You are a human and you are composed of energy and so is your soul. Being around a darker spirit's energy can affect your aura and how your body would deal with this energy or interpret is by causing something physical to translate that energy or feelings.

Therefore, many psychics, mediums, empaths often feel sick when they arrive to a place that is chalk full of nasty energy. The problem is that if you are unprotected or not sure how to rid and protect yourself of these energies you can become very ill. These energies and entities like to go through the body of the living or touch them. It's like a spiritual assault to your body. The problem is that when they are more advanced or intelligent spirits they have learned how to cause physical harm and sickness than other souls who are newly dead or don't know yet how to control their energy. Since they no longer have physical hands to scratch you, they use their energy to create these marks. Their energetic body can use the form of when they were living and just visualize their hands scratching you. Again, this requires for them to be advanced and they often learn by frequent attempts on how to manipulate energy.

If you suspect your home is haunted or you have something darker you can do several things to protect yourself. If the entity was one human and is just stuck and darker in nature try a subtle approach and you can talk to them out loud and simply explain you are not here to cause them harm. This is now your space and they don't belong here anymore. Then envision a door in front of you of white light and tell the spirit to go into the light. This will take some visualization or imagination. You can also gather a few selenite crystals and put them on the floor in the formation of a door or rectangle. This can be a circle too. Basically, you will want to create an opening and when you do this you can add some incense like frankincense or any other incense you prefer and ask them to step into the circle or doorway you have created and cross over. You may have to repeat this several times and it may have to be repeated because some spirits are going to be very reluctant. How will you know if they crossed over you ask? You will feel lighter, the atmosphere usually feel's better, you will notice activity ceases. After crossing over you should sage your entire home and say something like "I only allow love and light to fill this space. Nothing negative can stay." At least this is how I would do it but keep in mind there is no right or wrong way. You can say whatever you feel like as long as it is tailored to your taste and makes sense to you. It's important to note that you should say a prayer calling upon warrior angels like Archangel Michael to protect you and help you with crossing over souls before opening a door for them to cross over.

If the entity is weak you can sprinkle salt all around property, some prefer to use sea salt, or Himalayan salt. This should be placed all over the home and entry ways. Salt is for purification and also for protection. You can also light a white candle and call upon your angels to help protect you and ask the spirits or entities to cross over.

In some cases, you might have to be more forceful in your approach, but I would highly not recommend this especially if this has been going on for quite some time. If you don't feel comfortable doing any of the things mentioned above to rid yourself of these entities then you may need to call a paranormal team of experts, psychic or spiritual medium to help guide you on how to rid yourself of these darker energies. It's important to note here that darker energies can't stay in a place of love for long periods of time so a family that is really close, pisses them off if they are demonic or just darker energies. This is why many times they will prey among the weakest person in the family. This could be someone who has an addiction, who has something that they cannot control. Spirits can use this to spark arguments in the family, turn people who loved each other against themselves. They can target the strongest person too. Their main goal is to separate and conquer. Think about it, if everyone is fighting each other or arguing this creates a warm atmosphere of negativity. This is their domain and space. They love negativity and thrive on it. You take that away from their equation they have no ties to this physical world. Therefore, in things like possessions or the demonic, the demon will usually possess someone in the family or multiple people to wreak havoc and cause separations. It's not uncommon for families who are victims of such hauntings or energy often result in couples separating, divorce, legal issues, and even suicide in some cases.

Demons are harder to get rid of and if you have something demonic in your space, many people think that if they move that the demon will stay at the house because it is being haunted. This is a myth and in fact, once a link has been made with a living person, that demon will follow that person wherever they go. Think of them as your shadow. Basically, where you go, they go. People who are possessed usually look run down, very angry or out of it, catatonic at times, speaking in foreign languages, have hatred against holy objects, religious statues, holy water, scapular medals, animals will seem very afraid of this person, they will have a stench (usually rotten or decayed), will isolate themselves, complain they constantly hear a voice that speaks to them and is very negative in nature usually ordering them to cause harm to others living in the home, darker thoughts, seems to have clairvoyance when they never had this before (This is not to be confused with someone who is spiritually awakened and has abilities because a possessed person will have not just clairvoyance but the other symptoms mentioned above as well), etc.

Saint Benedictine medal is an exorcism medal and protects against the demonic and dark magic. If you haven't bought one it can also help against darker souls. Tread very carefully if you suspect demonic activity and know fear is their stomping ground. Take fear away and seek help through a demonologist or priest or pastor. These individuals will have more experience in dealing with these types of cases and can help you with the demonic. I will note that demonic cases are extremely rare, and some type of investigation must happen before a member of clergy will agree to assist in the case. Some tests such as psychological illnesses must be ruled out as well before an exorcism of the house or person is performed. Sometimes a priest can come and perform a house blessing, so the things outlined in this chapter do not describe every situation or experience.

There are different ways of handling situations, however, hopefully this chapter gives you a better understanding about what spirits can do.

Chapter 37

STUCK AFTER DEATH

Many clients have asked me how do we know if we are going to stay earthbound when we transition into spirit. We have heard a lot about earthbound spirits not crossing over to the other side, but we sometimes never stop for a minute and contemplate what causes us to stay trapped here on earth as an Earthbound spir- it. More importantly, what steps can you take to prevent from becoming earthbound? So, for those of you who may be reading this and think this sounds all like gibberish as you never have heard of the term Earthbound, I will ex- plain.

An earthbound spirit is a human soul that was once living here on earth and has now died and instead of see- ing the tunnel of light so many see, they have decided to stay here on earth because of unfinished business or oth- er reasons I will go into detail with. This doesn't mean that they did not see the light, many earthbound spirits in fact, have seen the light but fear it.

They fear judgment possibly for bad things they did here on earth and fear what they perceive to be purgatory or hell. They still remember their deeds and fear being held accountable but most of this punishment is self-inflicted and therefore they stay here on earth haunting people or wandering aimlessly in their familiar territories they used to live in.

As I've mentioned there are so many reasons they choose to stay earthbound but it's not a permanent state. Eventually their angels and guides will forcibly remove them to the other side, so they can begin to heal and basically understand their decisions, choices, actions, and everything they have done here in the physical world.

Now what are the chances you will stay earthbound when you pass if that time should come? This is the tricky question but it's quite simple! Here's a list of questions to ask yourself.

- Did I suffer any emotional, sexual, mental, physical trauma in my life and died without healing that?
- Do I have any grudges, anger, resentment, that I have not released?
- Do I have any secrets that I have never disclosed due to fear of being judged?
- Did I cause anyone else pain and never made amends or asked for forgiveness from this person?

Living here on earth is not easy and let's face it, not many of us will deal with issues that have happened to us in the same manner. Some of us have been served a cup

of tea full of strife, emotional pain and sometimes therapy, counseling, and spiritual healing doesn't always do the
trick. Depending on how deep our wounds are. So, if you
are worried about being stuck here after dying you need
to take steps while you are alive and not wait until the
last minute to address all of this. I know this may sound to
some like I'm coming from a place of fear but it's quite the
opposite. I would like to think I am providing you with an
awareness that will have you thinking about your current
choices, decisions, etc. There's no right or wrong answers.

Every case is different, but I want to provide you with
some ways to fix outstanding issues. Many people who
are terminal and their families can attest that often, it's
too late to say I'm sorry or make amends with everyone
who you hurt or who has hurt you before we pass.

The following is a list of things to do to ensure you
have a clear soul that isn't filled with unfulfilled things.

- Make sure you forgive those who hurt you even if
  you never forget but forgive them.
- If you hurt someone and wanted to say sorry but
  this person has passed, moved away, or you have
  no clue where they are then write a letter to this
  person asking for forgiveness then burn it. This
  will send it to the universe and out of you.
- You want to get everything you have been holding
  onto like regrets out and address those.
- Continuously work on yourself and controlling
  your emotions.

- Ask for forgiveness to anyone you feel you need it from.

- Get rid of bad habits that only hinder your life or impact others here.

- Tie up loose ends and always have a back up plan, if you don't finish something make sure someone else can carry it out for you.

If you can do these things before passing, you won't feel as if you have things that are left unfinished. The chances of you crossing over to the spirit realm is higher. Your soul will have known that it did its best and learned from its mistakes. Take the time you have here and now to make positive changes. When all is said and done, the money in your bank account, the house you and your family fought about, the will that never got found, and the secrets hidden will not matter. What will matter is the good deeds you did here on earth, how many people you helped, what you contributed as a living person here on earth. Use your time wisely and never lose a precious second living your dreams. If you first don't succeed at something do not stop, instead keep trying to get ahead.

Chapter 38

Dangers Mediums Face

For many who haven't yet awakened or are vibrating on the third dimension of consciousness it can be rather difficult to understand what a Spiritual Medium goes through. Many have a misconception and think that our connection to spirit is simple and that spirit gives us the answers and we share it with you. This is only part of what goes on. We often hear people say, "I wish I had your gift!" The reality is that being a Spiritual Medium has consequences as well. I'm writing this for many of you who have spiritually sensitive children, young mediums, and those of you where are beginning your journey as a medium. Yes, Mediums communicate with the dead. However, I will explain this better. We are like radios and have different channels through which spirit transfers their information to us, using signs, symbols, visions, words, smells, taste, touch, and feelings. As mediums we are like a light bulb and spirit sees this around us and they are attracted. It's like when you have a porch light on at night. Insects or bugs are attracted to it. Same applies to us.

As we do our sessions we must properly prepare ourselves and open ourselves to spirit. We do that by relaxing our mind. A busy mind filled with worries, focused on what you are preparing for dinner, errands you need to run, and other things will make the connection with spirit weak. You must be relaxed and the key to that is meditation, prayer and grounding yourself before a reading. Remember we are spiritual beings but we are human and have human bodies which are affected by spirit. Meditation helps us establish a connection with our higher self and to push everything else that is extra out. Some listen to music, some sit in a quiet space, some will draw, some will work on breathing techniques, and the list goes on and on. Grounding is also important to protecting yourself and I will explain why. When we are sensitives and have medium abilities, we are prone to attack, being physically ill, and developing unhealthy attachments.

I've heard someone in a forum once say, well I've been doing this for years and I don't need to meditate before I read, the trouble with that is that they are not going to be connected with their higher self and the universe so some of their insight might be confusing to them and their sitter (Person receiving the reading). We are not immune to spirit and the energy it requires. Grounding yourself can be done by meditation, it can be done holding a protective crystal, earthing (walking barefoot on the ground), or through prayer. When you do this, you are also needing to ensure you have a good connection with your guides. They will usually talk with you or give your insight. They aren't necessarily giving us the answers but do help during our session with spirit.

Now after that is done and we start reading for a client, we are channeling info from your passed loved one and our guides to bring forth any other information necessary. As mental or physical mediums we are often feeling DEATH pass through us. Let me repeat that again, we are feeling DEATH and processing it through our body. How can our connection to spirit affect us? It takes our energy, we use our physical energy and allow spirit to work through us. They are on a different frequency than us and we can feel their DEATH! How they died. So, let's say they passed from a suicide and hung themselves, we might feel severe head and neck pain in our body. If they passed from a heart attack, we would feel pressure in the chest, palpitations, or sharp pains. It's not our physical symptoms but rather spirit using their energy to make us feel how they passed and from what they passed.

So, it's that simple right? NO! Every session we do not only uses our energy but taxes our body. So, you might be asking if it's dangerous why are you in this link of work. The side effects if you protect yourself and open yourself up properly are minimal but we still feel sick at times and prone to getting illnesses more than the average person who is not in tune with their abilities. When you are done with a session it is important you CLOSE properly. What does closing means, it means that when we channel spirits, we open a doorway or gateway to the other side. It is like a little light around us through which spirit can walk in at any given moment. Sometimes what comes through are negative energies as well. This is why we need to close ourselves. This is not to be misconstrued by thinking we can shut off our gift because it's not. We will always have the gift and it will be there, but you want to shut the door that would allow yourself to pick up spirit anywhere you go.

Because spirit is always around their loved ones, homes, places you visit an etc. To close yourself you can visualize yourself in a bubble of white light, you can visualize a door shut in your third eye, you can say a protective prayer in your own words basically saying, "I now shut all doors to the other side for now, please respect my space." You can also sage after a session with someone. This will help protect yourself from being susceptible to attachments or etc.

So, when we are in constant contact with spirit but not aware that they are around we can start to develop anxiety attacks, panic attacks. These are signs spirit is around you and tapping at you like if they were at a door knocking. They are trying to tell you that they are there. Many mediums will suppress their abilities and know that there is NO method to completely shut them out and in turn feel anxiety or panic attacks. Also, since we are channeling death, we are more prone to developing heart issues, weight issues, unexplained or chronic pain, and lose sleep. Basically, we can have many other illnesses and even Near-Death Experiences. Some physical mediums don't live long lives because of this.

As I've said there are many ways to manage your abilities through working with stones, tai chi, yoga, meditation, prayer. For those of us who are sensitives and have abilities if you have issues like anger built in, past hurt you haven't been able to deal with or something traumatic. This can make you more susceptible to spiritual attacks and illnesses. You need to deal with these emotions and protect yourself by following what I outlined above or develop your own list of routines to use. Every medium is different, and every medium will open and close a session however they feel. I am only sharing this as I have been using my opening and closing techniques for some time now, and they WORK! You will notice a change.

For those of you who are sitters, I think this chapter will give you a better perspective from what we do. If you have a child who you suspect has medium abilities or psychic abilities know that in most cases they are not imagining or suffer from a mental illness. If they tell you they hear spirit, they hear voices, they see things or if they draw this in their drawings, please know this is very REAL! Children often get misdiagnosed and put on medicines that continue to suppress them and hinder their God given abilities. Not every person with natural born abilities will necessary go into this line of work but can use their abilities as a guide to navigate this world. Some say it's a blessing or curse but essentially you were either born with it or developed it as a latent ability for a purpose. To serve humanity.

If you are a medium who is interested in doing readings, remember to not burn yourself out.

Do only a certain amount of sessions a day. There is always tomorrow. These were wise words that were given to me when I embarked on this journey and didn't realize until I experienced some minor issues later. You must treat your body as your temple and know without it, you can't do your spiritual work to the best of your abilities. Set up boundaries at night and let Spirit know that you are going to sleep, this is your space and time and they can go to someone else who is open for business! You're not being rude but making sure they know how you feel. YOU are in CONTROL! It's your body and abilities they are using to communicate through. If you have children who have medium or spiritual abilities, give them a night light, give them a flashlight or something that makes them feel protected. Help them by giving them a prayer to say at night. It can be a prayer as simple as praying to GOD, Jesus, or even their Guardian angels and letting spirit know in their nightly prayers that they are not to disturb them and go to someone else who is open.

Educate them that they have nothing to be afraid of and to be empowered. They also would benefit from keeping a dream journal or any journal and release their thoughts and dreams in it. As parents of children with abilities, it might be beneficial for you to do the same, so you can properly release your emotions. It's not easy, there's no handbook or manual to prepare for this. Just be a support system and listen.

Chapter 39

Symptoms of a Love Spell

I chose to write this because while many still don't believe in the POWER of witchcraft it is very real and is often used by men and women to hold onto someone who they want for themselves for whatever reasons. Sometimes they have feelings for this person, sometimes the other person is oblivious and has no signs, sometimes they are just there for the money and want to be with this person. Whatever the case is, doing a love spell or going to a witch to have one done is something that has become more common than you think. It's like a dirty little secret that most won't confess to but when you come across a psychic, trust me we may not say what you did but know what you did.

Many come to us with love issues and wonder why their relationship is horrible, why they separated, why the other person suddenly stopped loving them. The REAL question is why you felt you could manipulate someone without letting their free will guide them to you? There is always CONSEQUENCES for the person who has done the spell which I will cover both. If you are a witch or just dabbling and you do a love spell to call love to you and attract Love this is not what I'm calling out in this chapter. That is okay because you are just asking the universe and elements to help you bring love or for you to find love. This is more for those who are consciously aware of their actions and taking it upon their hands to stay in a relationship by force or using force to obtain something that is not natural.

Here is a list of things people who want to do a love spell may take from their intended victim. This is just a minimal list but there may be more things that I haven't listed.

Typically, they will obtain the following:

- *A personal item belonging to this person such as article of clothing, undergarment, object they use*
- *A hairbrush (they use the hair in the brush for their spell)*
- *A photograph of the person*
- *Handwriting from the person (this could be your signature, letter, anything with your handwriting)*
- *Jewelry or Accessories (Watch, earrings, necklace, bracelet, necktie, cuff links, handkerchief, etc.)*
- *Tooth brush*
- *Toenail clippings*
- *Body Fluids (Saliva, fecal matter, and the list goes on) including combining their own body*

fluids with yours! (TMI I know and fully apologize for this graphic content, but knowledge is power).

Next what they do with these items is to usually use a photograph or poppet in combination with these items. They will use a red string or cord (color of string doesn't matter) to attach your personal item to the photo or poppet. The poppet represents you. Then they focus their intent and energy on you with a combination of a spell recited to force their victim to only be with them or love them. They use typically red candles because red is the color of love, but they can use different colors. They might have other things on their altar. If they are using a poppet or photograph they will hide this from you as they don't want, you to see it! They will hide it in a closet, drawer, box, in the shed, garage, or like the older generations would do, have a hole in the ground where they place the objects. They must cover their tracks.

If someone is using a love spell on you, you would feel the following:

- *Hated or disliked this person initially but now find them fascinating and you can't explain it but love them.*

- *You begin to have nightmares usually this person will be in your dreams, or you may see your loved ones in harm.*

- *You will begin to develop severe anxiety and panic attacks (Your body is picking up unnatural spiritual magic being used against you.)*

- *You become obsessive about them and think about them even when you don't want to think about them. You just can't seem to get them out of your mind.*

- *You might be in public and begin to see them in other people or see their face wherever you are.*

- *You start drawing away from your closest friends and family members (they might even notice you would always make time to spend with them, but you suddenly have drawn away from them)*

- *Arguments with loved ones usually about the person who has done a love spell on them will occur. If you have family members with spiritual abilities, they will feel this union is unnatural and even tell you that they feel that magic is being used against you. You will NOT agree and think it's just their imagination. Trust me your family may know you better than you know yourself and know that you are not attracted to this type of person.*

- *Your relationship is more sexual in nature, but you don't share any other interests that they do.*

- *The witch or person doing the spell may wrap a piece of your hair in their hair or carry* it on them.

Other things to watch out for:

- *Witches who are doing spells on you may seem very friendly to you but every time that you come around them, they want to feed you or give you something to drink (Potions with their own body fluid, hair or just liquids they have hexed are added to the food or drinks. Be very aware and deny the food. Notice their reaction. Many will become offended or subtly change their attitude because they wanted you to take this, so they could essentially "poison and hex" you with continued magic.*

- *See they don't just do this once, they must keep their magic going so they will continue to do this.*

- *They might see something new like a new or old piece of jewelry and say that they absolutely love it. You might feel compelled to give it to them, you might be asked by the witch if they can borrow it and that they will give it back to you! BAD IDEA! Don't do it. Bewitchment can be put on the object and be given back to you.*

- *They might tell you that they forgot their jacket or sweater, can they borrow yours.*

- *They might ask for your hairbrush or something as simple as something you touched. (They know no limits).*

If you suspect that you are a victim of someone's love spell you can do the following:

- *Use a Saint Benedictine Medal and wear it al-ways either as a pendant form or in your pock-*

et, purse or wallet. This medal protects against harmful witchcraft, evil, etc.

- *You can also use salt and take a bath with it in a tub. Like Scrubbing yourself (aura) clean from it.*

- *You can visit a reiki master to get a healing and remove any cords done. If you have any objects, clothing from this person who used to share space with you.... throw their things away.*

- *Get rid of everything even gifts given to you. They might have energy still attached to those objects.*

- *If they slept on your bed, wash all the linen and sage your mattress and put a bowl of salt under the bed on the floor. Salt is for purification. If you have a saint Benedictine medal put one in between the mattress and the box spring.*

- *Use selenite tumbled stone and put one on each corner of the bedroom to create a barrier of protection.*

- *Prayer is very helpful, and you can also wear amulets like the evil eye (Hamas), crucifix, etc.*

No magic is strong enough that it will last forever, this is what witches don't realize.

As I've mentioned before there are consequences for both the person who has done the love spell or if they went to a witch there is consequences for them as well. The universe and Karma always hold you accountable for your dirty deeds. No amount of magic regardless of how powerful you believe you are can help you. When you play with magic you are using spirits, evil entities and more calling upon energy from mother earth to force something that is NOT written.

Here are some things you would experience:

- *Your victim which you cast a spell upon to love you, stops loving you and now hates you and wants nothing to do with you.*

- *You notice your health is deteriorating (you took energy from sources to force something, now it's time to pay up. You will notice the universe and spirit begin to take energy from YOU!) It's an even exchange.*

- *Pets may begin to mysteriously get sick and die.*

- *Loved ones can develop illnesses (someone who you love deeply in your family, because it's an exchange of love) this can lead to death in many cases. It depends on how long you have done this for and how many times you did it.*

- *You begin to develop nightmares (usually darker ones).*

- *You begin to be attacked in your home (seeing dark shadows, lights flickering, smelling a rotten smell, hearing growls.)*

- *You may begin to see bugs and maggots in your home. Infestation of some sort will occur. Mice or Rats may begin to appear.*

- *Objects and jewelry may begin to break.*

- *You could now be the one having panic attacks and feel scared or paranoid.*
- *Since the heart is the object of love, you might develop heart issues.*
- *Your own loved ones may turn against you and delete you from their life*
- *Your closest friend's breakup with you and want nothing to do with you.*

This list goes on and one. The key here is to know if you invoke magic to obtain the object of your affection and it's not natural there is a price to pay. Spirits and the earth is not there to do your bidding but to co-exist. Other magic that is white magic and used to protect yourself, using herbs for healing, does not have consequences. Essentially you are giving back to earth in some form not taking from the earth. There is balance in white magic. A love spell may seem like white magic, but it isn't. It's love magic!

Chapter 40

Unborn Souls & Young Souls Departed

For those of you who are struggling with the loss of your unborn baby or have lost a baby whether it made it full term or died shortly after giving birth, or even losing a young child my heart goes out to you first and foremost. It is one of the most painful experiences someone can ever endure and there are so many fears and insecurities that cross mom and dad.

Mothers usually grieve the loss and feel guilty or responsible or they could have done something to prevent this from occurring. The first thing I want to say is that we don't have control over anyone's passing. It all occurs as it should and even though it may seem unfair or cruel to us because we are human beings here on earth this is one of the hardest things to endure.

There's a lot of questions as well such as if a woman has a miscarriage was there a soul in the baby and what happened to it. Yes, there was a soul even if it was a few hours in your womb or months. A soul was assigned to this mom to be to be born. However, the soul of this child either chose to not be born because it was not the right time for the parents, or the child will be born at a later time to the same parents (soul recycling), the stay was temporary but had some impact on all the family sometimes causing partners to split up to be with other soul families or bring them closer together. The soul of a miscarriage may also have had to go through this temporary visit for karmic reasons. The soul of the baby may be called back as well if it knows the parents will not be together long term. Meaning some people are not married when this happens. Some are married but have existing issues leading up to the birth. A soul may choose not to be born because the birth could result in complications leading up to the passing of the mother during childbirth and it's not her time to leave this physical world because she has a family already and other children who need her.

You must understand the possibilities of why souls stay for longer or shorter periods of time on earth all depends on the soul's evolution. How many lessons it has learned. You also have to remember most souls, have been here many lifetimes so although this is a new body or new baby growing inside of you, the soul has no age only lifetimes. It's not governed by a number like we define ourselves here on earth. We use time here on earth. It time does not exist in the spirit world.

All unborn babies/infant's souls go straight to heaven. The souls of children who pass at a young age may decide to stay here as earthbound spirits to watch over the family. They may not realize their family has moved on but they always have their personal angel from the other side there with them. Sometimes they are allowed to stay with their parents or cross over but usually they don't stay in a period for a long time as they will cross over to reconnect with their family in heaven. If an earthbound child stays behind they may give you signs like move their toys, you may hear a child's cries, giggles, laughter, handprints or footprints, see their shadows, or other experiences.

Unborn babies and young children do not feel any pain even if their passing was a result of traumatic event. These souls may come up in readings and these souls if they stayed on the other side to watch over their parents on earth they can grow in heaven. Sometimes in a reading a medium/psychic may see the miscarriage or know if occurred as they could see the child in spirit or a fetus if it was a baby. Sometimes they will see colors of the gender even if the parents didn't know what would have been the gender of the baby. So let's say you lost a pregnancy due to miscarriage the child was never born but they can continue to grow in the other side so if a reader tells you they see a little girl of 5 years it could be 5 years since the child's passing or it could have been 2 years but the child has grown in the spirit world or presented themselves to a psychic or medium in this manner to let you know they are fine and okay. Remember the soul has really no age or number yes it may be an old soul but it can show itself any the way you would connect to or understand.

It's not rare for mothers or fathers to see the child or have an unborn baby appear as a toddler or slightly older version in their dreams. Some parents may recognize this soul to be their child, while others may not have a clue until a reader points this out.

If you've experienced the loss of a child know that they are okay and with you. We all transform and will connect or reconnect with them at some point. Be strong and know you are loved.

Chapter 41

CRYSTAL POWER

For those of you who have been following me and supporting me it will come as no surprise that I am a lover of crystals and I work with them to heal myself and others out there. I always suggest certain ones to certain clients because every case is different, and one crystal can be used for multiple reasons. However, I want to talk about a few that are so important to me and which I have worked with for some years now.

When I was first introduced to crystals it was going through Instagram and seeing posts about them. At first, I was like it's just a rock how can that help me? Then I read threads and comments by others, and I was surprised by this fascination. I therefore embarked on a journey to collect as many as I could. I now have close to a hundred crystals but mini ones. I am still saving to add some larger ones that weigh about 3-7 lbs.

I learned early on as well the best crystal choices are the ones that you can purchase at a local crystal shop if you have one. Sometimes they are overpriced but holding crystals in your hand and seeing how you feel immediately will help you determine which crystals are good for you. Since I didn't have that convenience as my town does not have these crystal shops I had to use my intuition and feel the energetic connection that exists on the spiritual plane and physical plane. Meaning I felt a connection to the object online. After receiving several kinds of crystals each one to me was special and made me feel different.

Some of my favorite crystals are Lapis Lazuli, Citrine, Quartz, Black Tourmaline, Turquoise, and Peridot. Heck I LOVE all crystals, but these are my absolute favorite ones! With Lapis Lazuli I felt this immediate warmth and I noticed it enhanced a lot of my psychic abilities instantaneously. It also helped me feel as if a lot of the negativity that we often absorb in public environments was shielded from me.

Citrine naturally is yellow and if it's orange in color this is actual amethyst that was heated and transformed and often called Citrine but it's amethyst. Citrine is pale yellow to dark yellow but some inclusions of clear quartz and transparency. This stone is a stone that doesn't have to be charged by the moonlight or sun because it has properties that enhance other crystals but also protects against negativity and can cleanse itself. It's quite remarkable. So, let's say you are going through issues in your job and looking for another job or you are having issues with debt/finances are not good. Then this stone is for you! I like to light a green candle when focusing on healing and abundance. I usually will take a dollar bill or $20-dollar bill and place it under the candle and have a piece of citrine by it. To amplify my petition and energy being sent into the universe.

Quartz is a clear stone and kind of silly to think we have this in our homes most often found in watches, computers, clocks, and other things. However, this was my first crystal that I EVER bought, and it is known as a master crystal. This crystal has the power to amplify all other crystals as well and fight negativity. It brings one clarity and can also help psychic abilities and remove blockages in your spiritual self. This is one that I would always carry with me. Being that it is clear it can also enhance your communication with angels and higher beings in the spiritual realm.

Black Tourmaline is one that I am in LOVE with. LOL Silly to think how can one LOVE one stone so much? Being in this line of work, I'm often the subject to dark energies and psychic attacks sent from other dark workers who also work in the spiritual community but work with darkness and dark magic. I've had so many of these attacks, but my black tourmaline is specifically perfect to block witchcraft being sent your way, negative energy, psychic attack, warding off psychic vampires, and the list goes on. I don't go out without a piece of this in my pocket! I mean I've had the evil eye sent my way and it made me sick before. It was the one time I didn't carry my black tourmaline with me. Ever since, I normally feel grounded with it and protected. Psychic attacks will still come through as not every crystal can prevent these things, but it can help to protect and reduce the frequencies of that energy.

Turquoise is one which I love because of the color and reminds me of the heavens and ocean. Plus, I have Native American blood and Native Americans worked highly with this crystal for healing. There is a lot of balance this crystal brings to one's life. It is calm and soothing for me. I feel like it can transform my moods as well. I recommend this crystal to anyone who is having back issues, health issues, sickness of any kind, and those who are going through breakups, heartbreak, loss, grieving. It can help you in all those aspects.

Peridot is special to me because although my birthstone is also green in color and darker (emerald), I felt more connection to Peridot. It's light green in color but it helps against psychic attacks, magic, and is transformative in many ways. It also is a stone of healing, but many have learned the power of this crystal.

One other stone which is often called a Crystal is Moldavite. It's a tektite type of glass that was created when a meteor hit earth millions of years ago and formed with the earth. This occurred in the Czech Republic and this is where the only pieces of Moldavite come from. If anyone else says Moldavite came from mines or was simulated in other parts of the world, this is NOT authentic Moldavite. I have worked with this stone for about a year now and it's amazing in all sense of the words. It can really push your life in directions that are unexpected but aligning you with your true path and transforming your life for the better. Its intense energy can make one sick a little at first, so you may have to go through periods of wearing it or having it on you for a few hours and then taking it off or setting it somewhere and then come back to it. It is rumored to be part of the Emerald tablets as well. All I know is that I often recommend this to clients who have been struggling a lot and really are seeking change. This stone seems to know your inner desires, so if you are willing to fight for change and want it, this is a POWERFUL stone to work with.

CPSIA information can be obtained
at www.ICGtesting.com
Printed in the USA
BVHW031408200720
584155BV00008B/92